SALT WATER TAFFY

~ THE SEASIDE ADVENTURES OF ~

JACK AND **BENNY**

CALDERA'S REVENGE

PART 2

Written & Illustrated by

MATTHEW LOUX

Lettered by **DOUGLAS E. SHERWOOD**
Edited by **JILL BEATON**
Design by **MATTHEW LOUX** *&* **TROY LOOK**

Oni Press, Inc.
publisher, Joe Nozemack
editor in chief, James Lucas Jones
marketing director, Cory Casoni
art director, Keith Wood
operations director, George Rohac
editor, Jill Beaton
editor, Charlie Chu
digital prepress lead, Troy Look

1305 SE Martin Luther King Jr. Blvd.
Suite A
Portland, OR 97214

www.onipress.com

First Edition: December 2011
978-1-934964-63-7

1 3 5 7 9 10 8 6 4 2

Library of Congress Control Number: 2011906143

Printed in U.S.A.

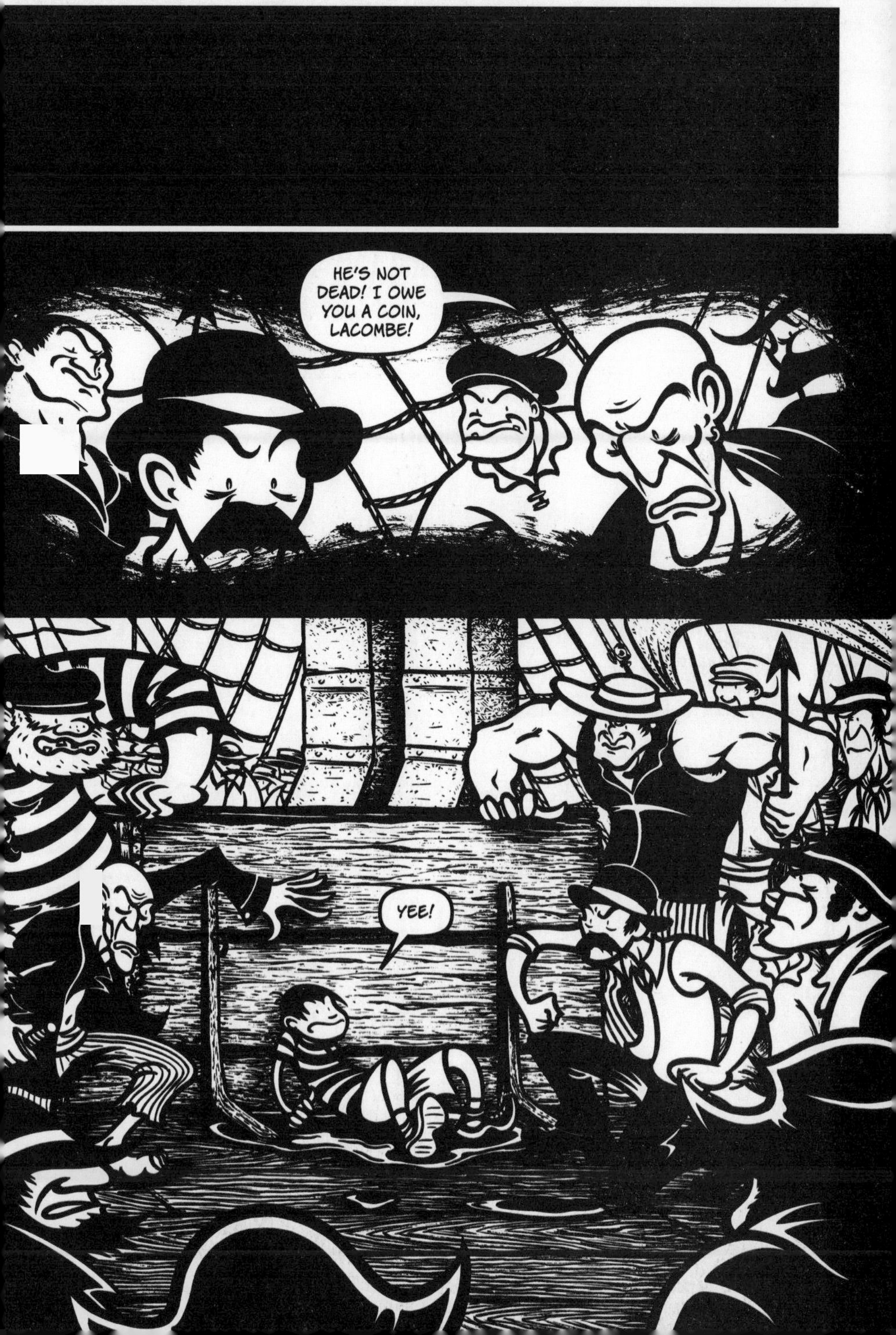
HE'S NOT DEAD! I OWE YOU A COIN, LACOMBE!
YEE!

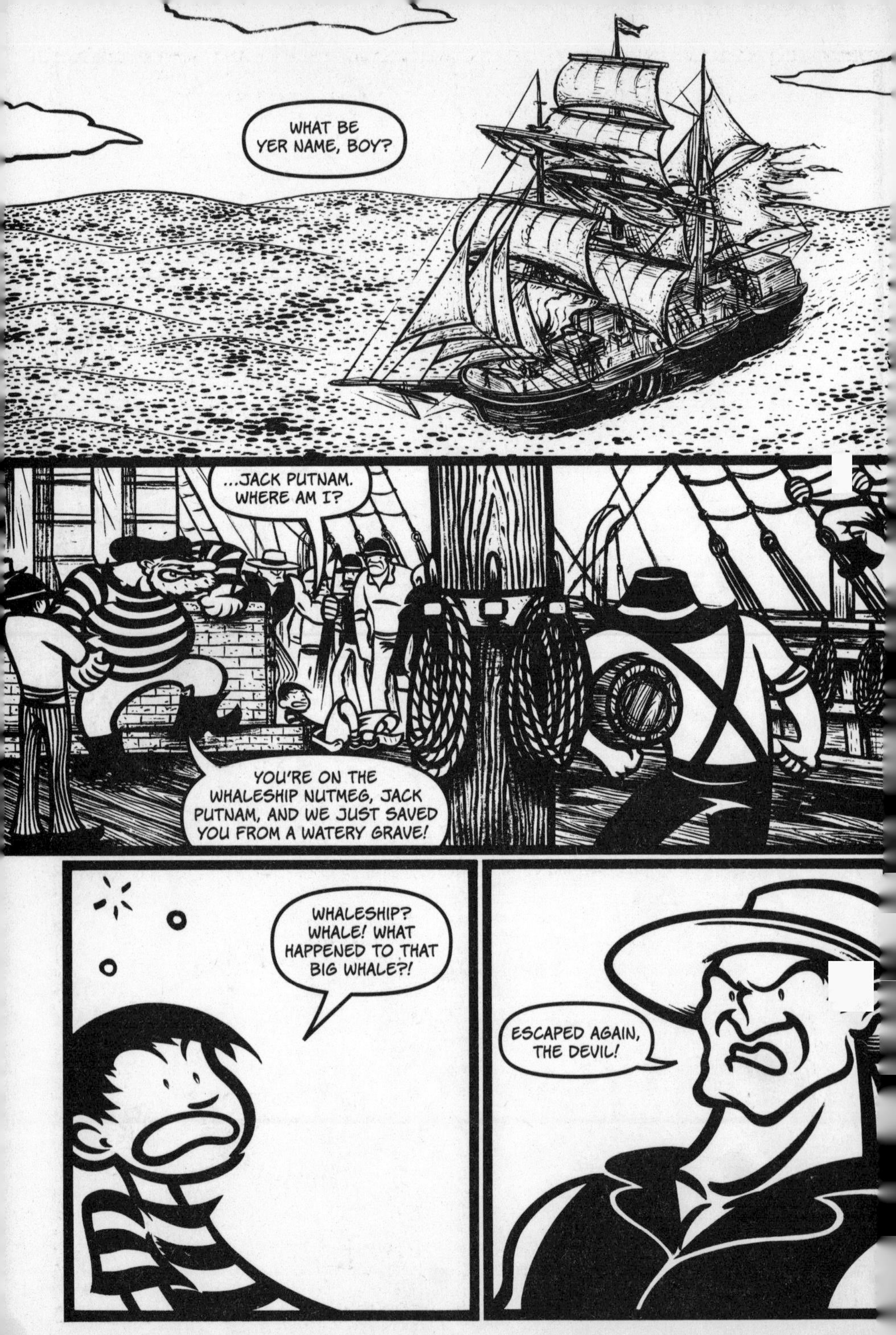
WHAT BE YER NAME, BOY?
...JACK PUTNAM. WHERE AM I?
YOU'RE ON THE WHALESHIP NUTMEG, JACK PUTNAM, AND WE JUST SAVED YOU FROM A WATERY GRAVE!
WHALESHIP? WHALE! WHAT HAPPENED TO THAT BIG WHALE?!
ESCAPED AGAIN, THE DEVIL!

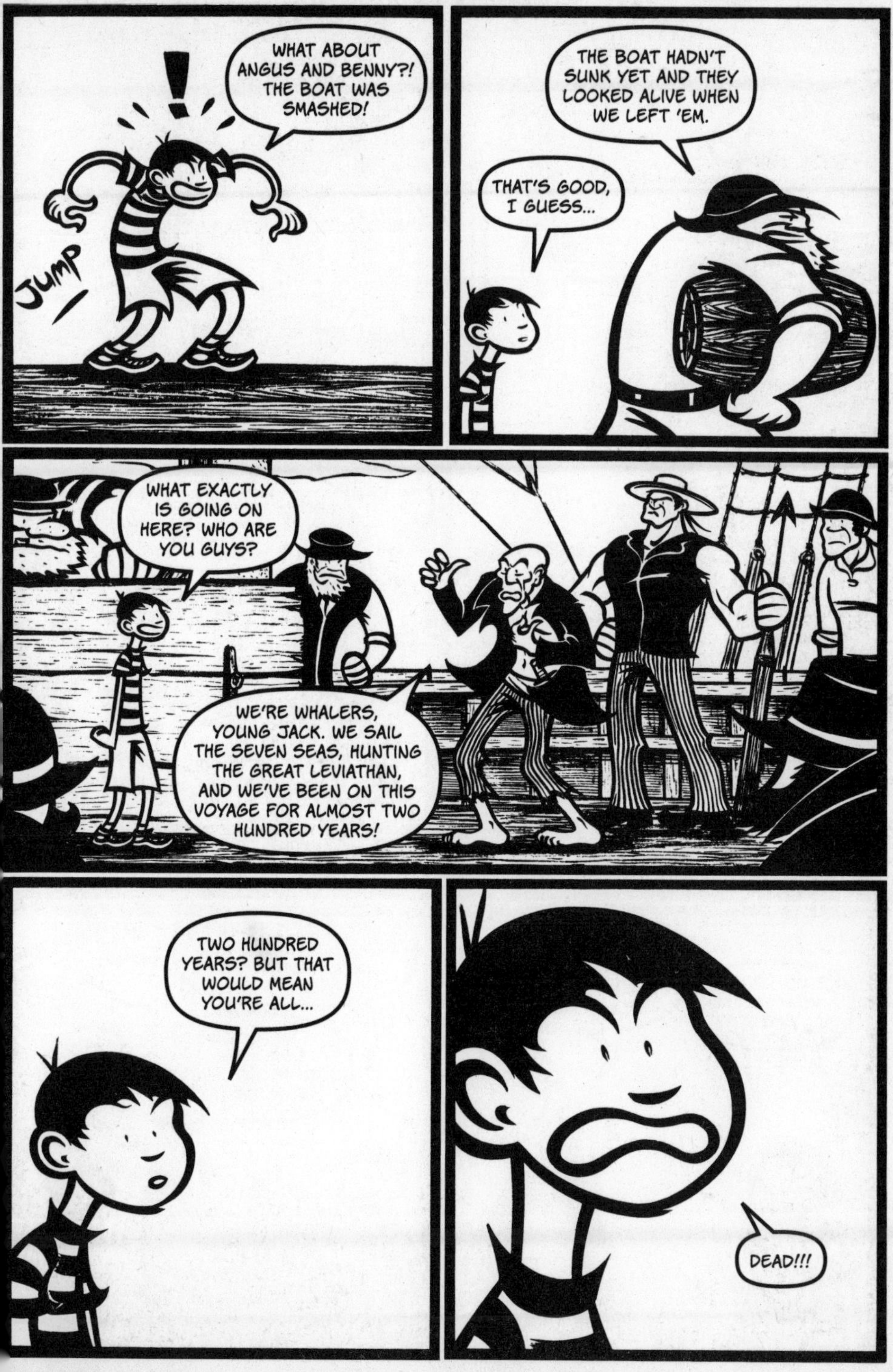

WHAT ABOUT ANGUS AND BENNY?! THE BOAT WAS SMASHED!
JUMP
THE BOAT HADN'T SUNK YET AND THEY LOOKED ALIVE WHEN WE LEFT 'EM.
THAT'S GOOD, I GUESS...
WHAT EXACTLY IS GOING ON HERE? WHO ARE YOU GUYS?
WE'RE WHALERS, YOUNG JACK. WE SAIL THE SEVEN SEAS, HUNTING THE GREAT LEVIATHAN, AND WE'VE BEEN ON THIS VOYAGE FOR ALMOST TWO HUNDRED YEARS!
TWO HUNDRED YEARS? BUT THAT WOULD MEAN YOU'RE ALL...
DEAD!!!

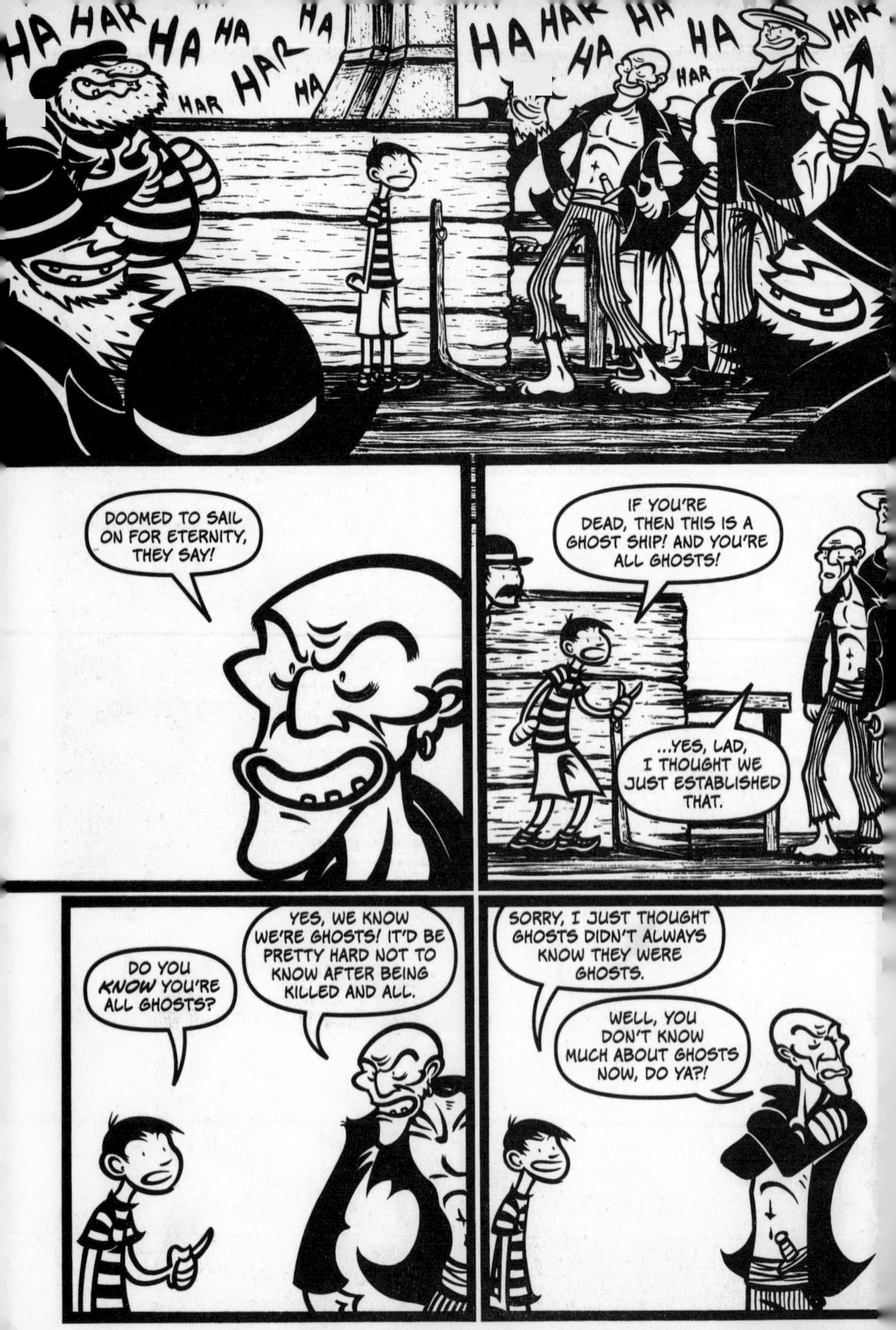
HA HAR HA HA HA HAR HAR HA
HA HAR HA HA HA HAR HAR
DOOMED TO SAIL ON FOR ETERNITY, THEY SAY!
IF YOU'RE DEAD, THEN THIS IS A GHOST SHIP! AND YOU'RE ALL GHOSTS!
...YES, LAD, I THOUGHT WE JUST ESTABLISHED THAT.
DO YOU *KNOW* YOU'RE ALL GHOSTS?
YES, WE KNOW WE'RE GHOSTS! IT'D BE PRETTY HARD NOT TO KNOW AFTER BEING KILLED AND ALL.
SORRY, I JUST THOUGHT GHOSTS DIDN'T ALWAYS KNOW THEY WERE GHOSTS.
WELL, YOU DON'T KNOW MUCH ABOUT GHOSTS NOW, DO YA?!

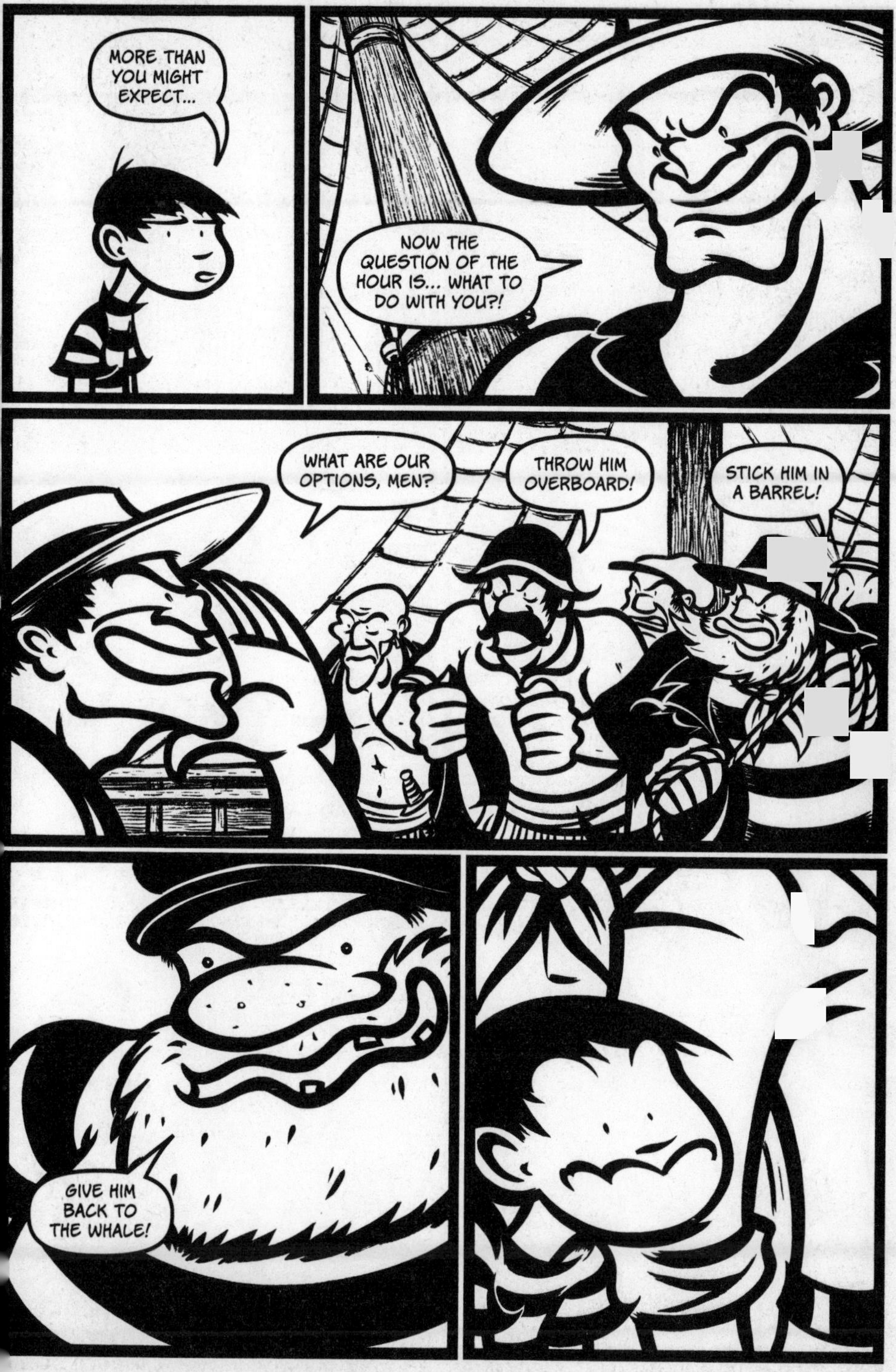
MORE THAN YOU MIGHT EXPECT...
NOW THE QUESTION OF THE HOUR IS... WHAT TO DO WITH YOU?!
WHAT ARE OUR OPTIONS, MEN?
THROW HIM OVERBOARD!
STICK HIM IN A BARREL!
GIVE HIM BACK TO THE WHALE!

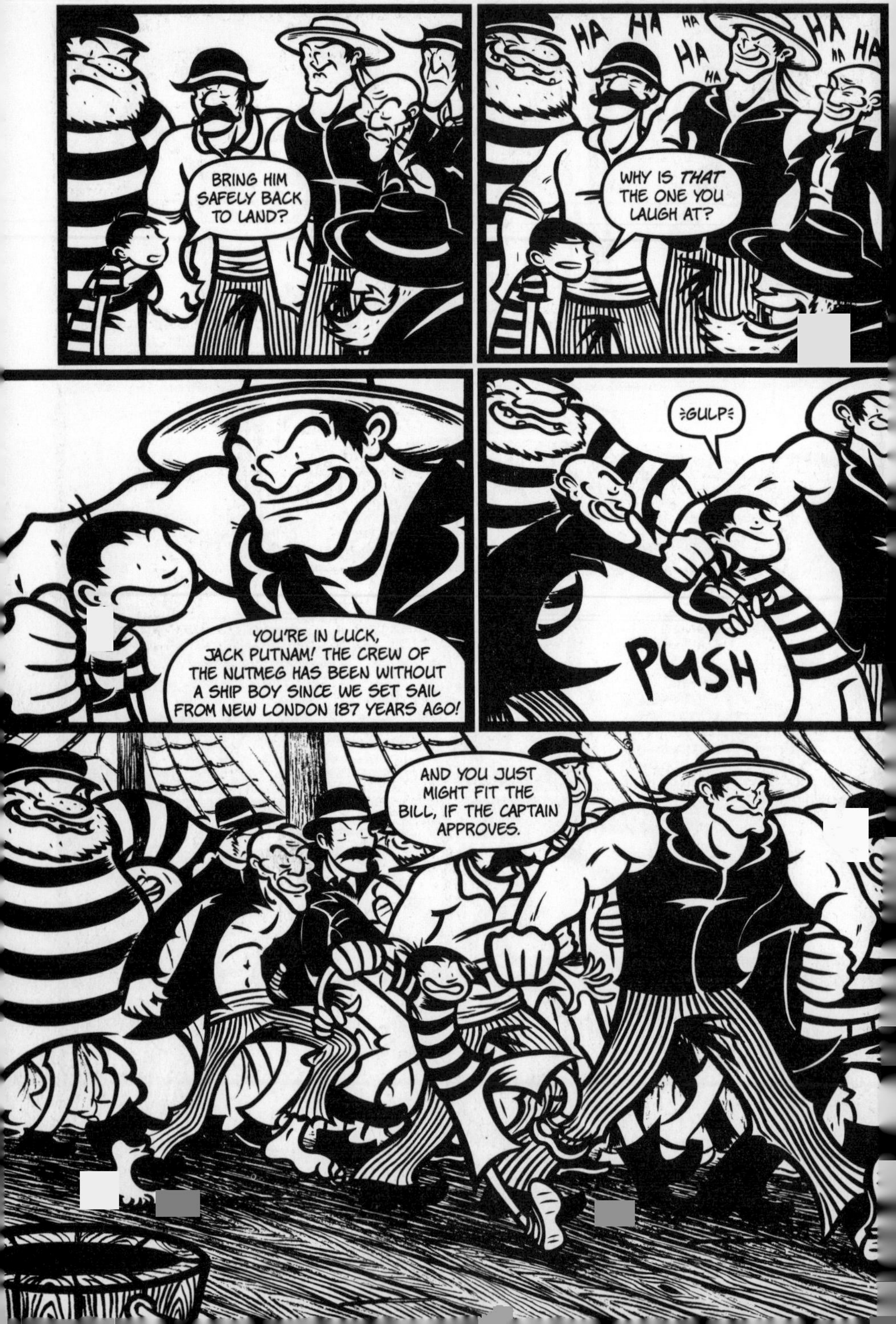
BRING HIM SAFELY BACK TO LAND?
HA HA HA HA HA HA HA HA HA
WHY IS THAT THE ONE YOU LAUGH AT?
YOU'RE IN LUCK, JACK PUTNAM! THE CREW OF THE NUTMEG HAS BEEN WITHOUT A SHIP BOY SINCE WE SET SAIL FROM NEW LONDON 187 YEARS AGO!
GULP
PUSH
AND YOU JUST MIGHT FIT THE BILL, IF THE CAPTAIN APPROVES.

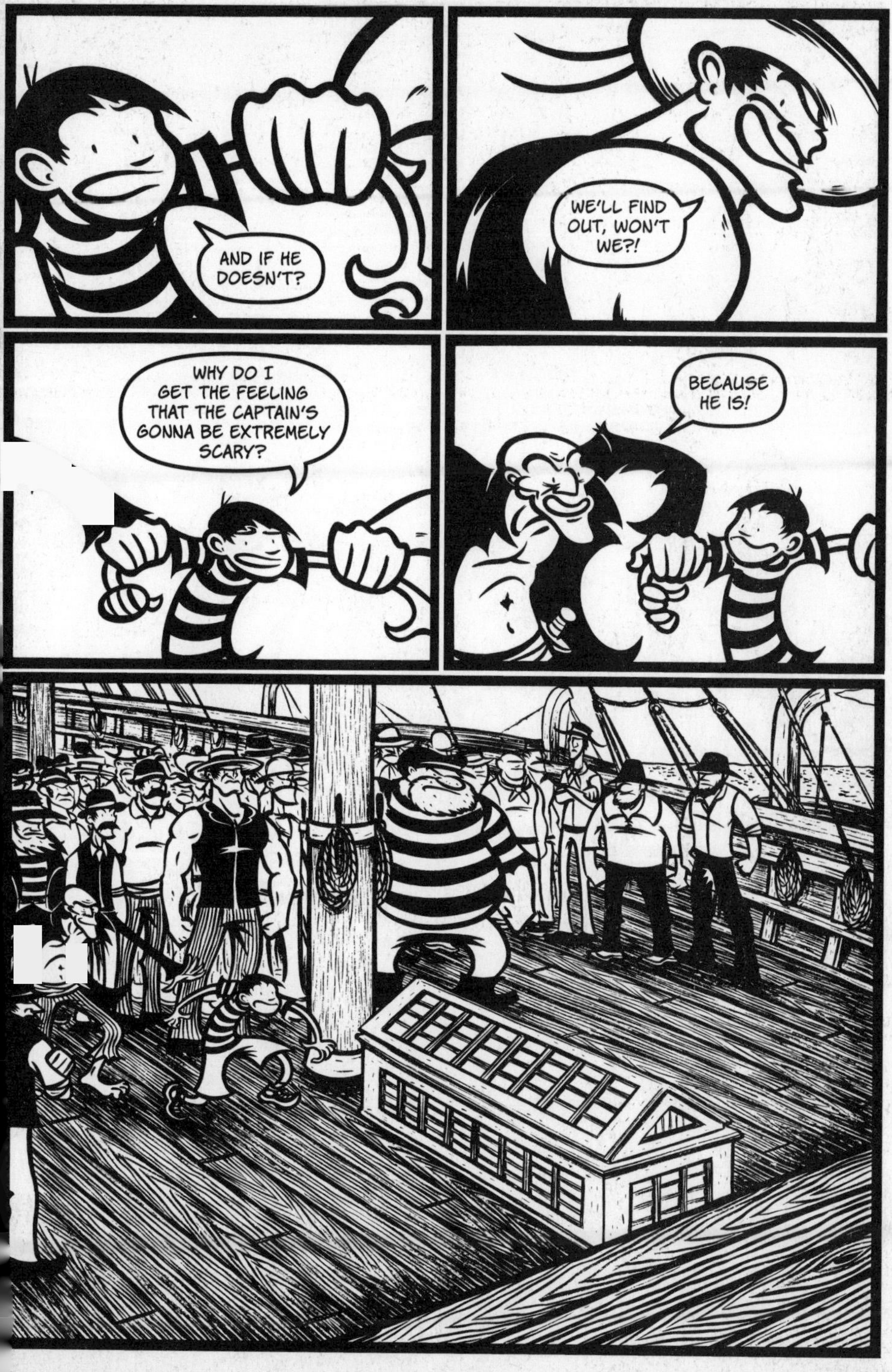
AND IF HE DOESN'T?
WE'LL FIND OUT, WON'T WE?!
WHY DO I GET THE FEELING THAT THE CAPTAIN'S GONNA BE EXTREMELY SCARY?
BECAUSE HE IS!

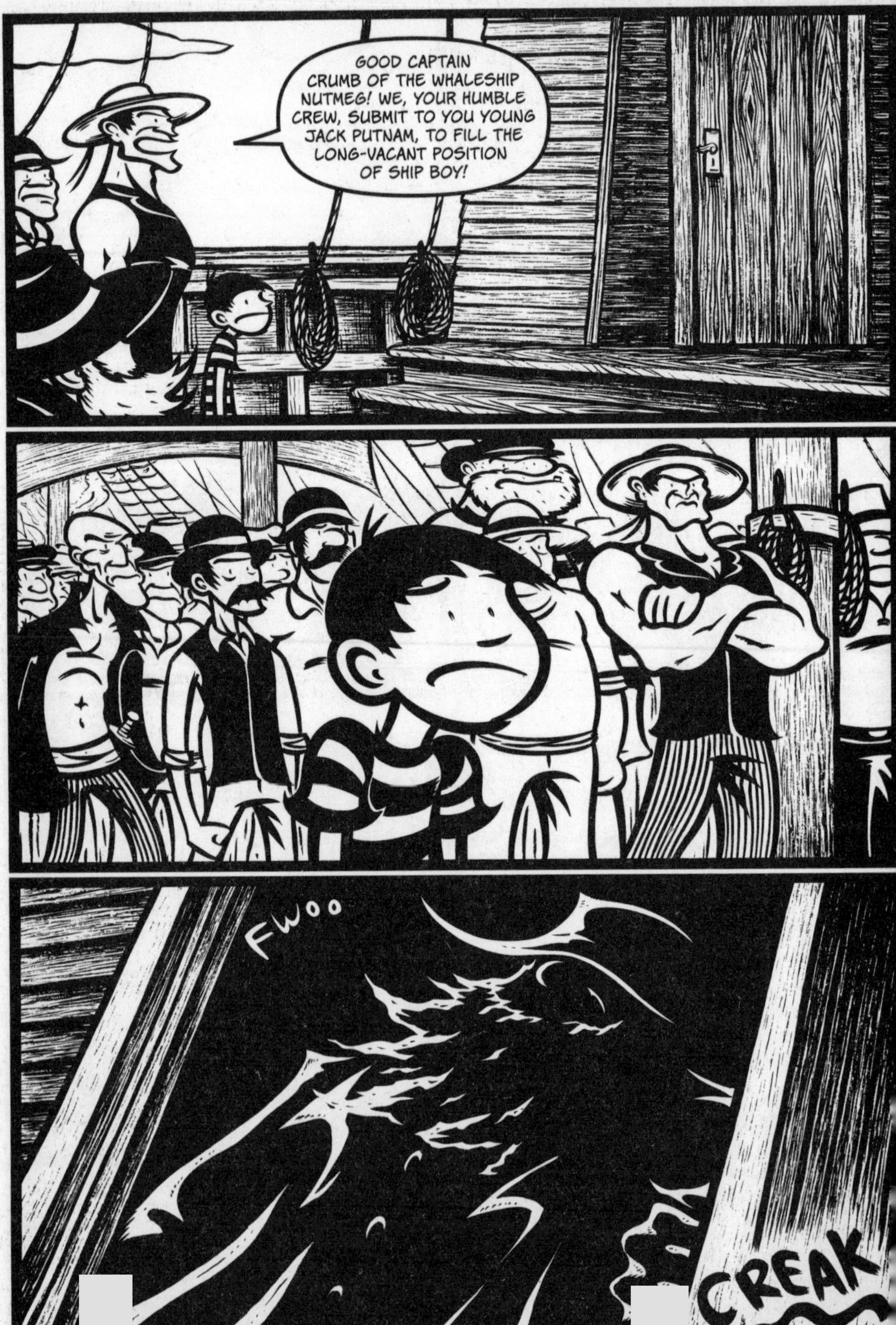
GOOD CAPTAIN CRUMB OF THE WHALESHIP NUTMEG! WE, YOUR HUMBLE CREW, SUBMIT TO YOU YOUNG JACK PUTNAM, TO FILL THE LONG-VACANT POSITION OF SHIP BOY!
FWOO
CREAK

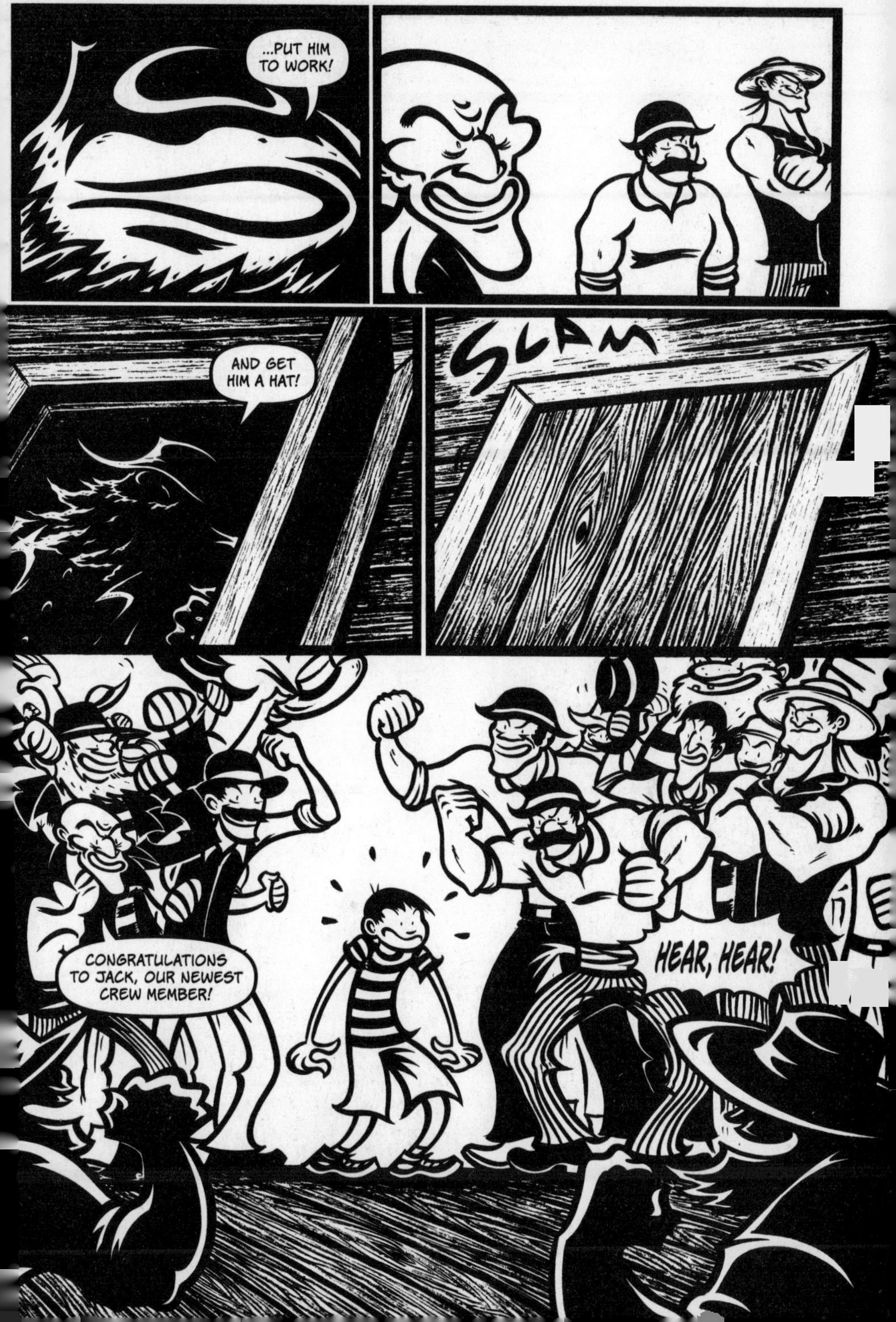
...PUT HIM TO WORK!
AND GET HIM A HAT!
SLAM
CONGRATULATIONS TO JACK, OUR NEWEST CREW MEMBER!
HEAR, HEAR!

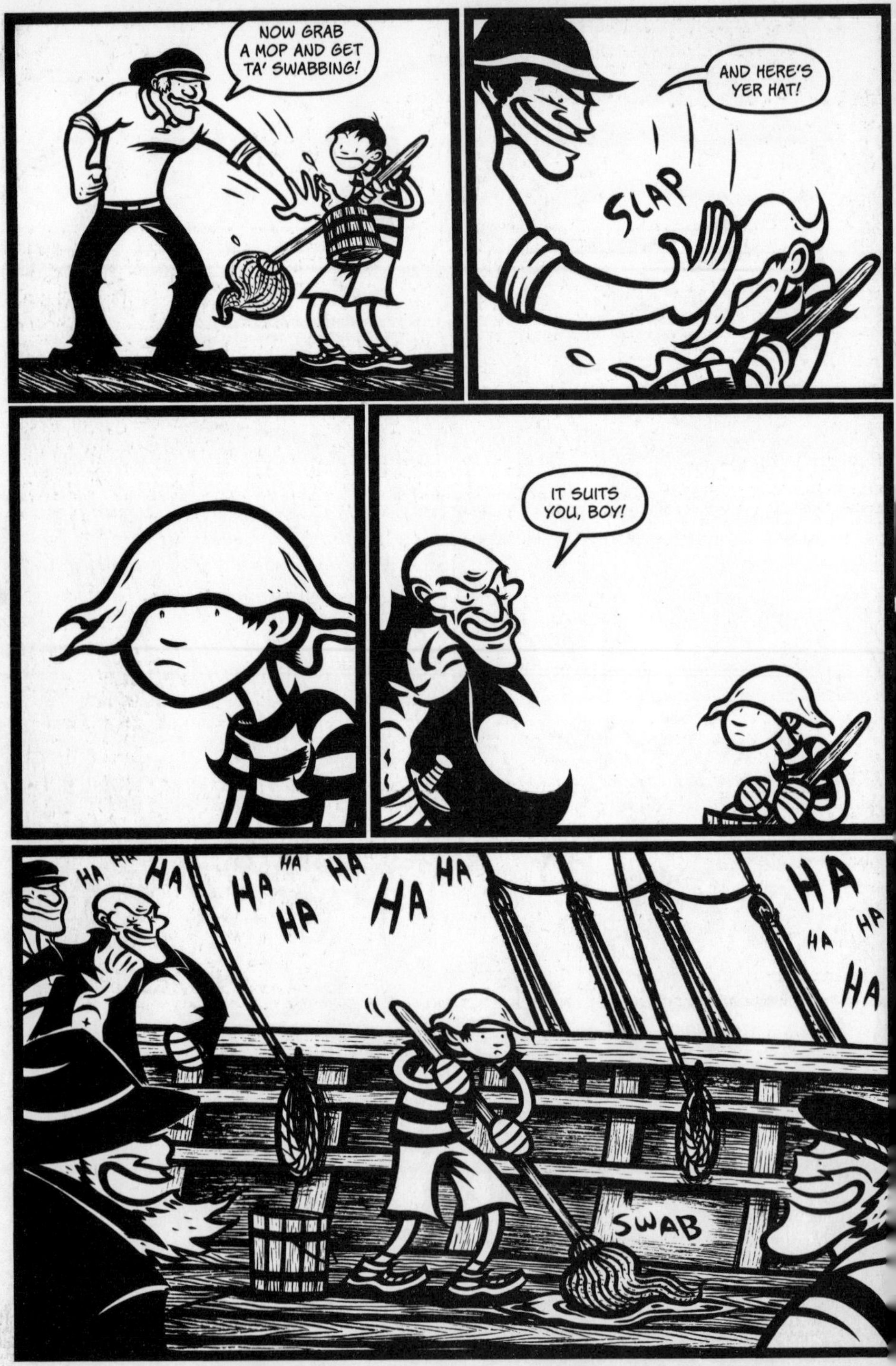
NOW GRAB A MOP AND GET TA' SWABBING!
AND HERE'S YER HAT!
SLAP
IT SUITS YOU, BOY!
HA HA HA HA HA HA HA HA HA HA HA HA HA HA
SWAB

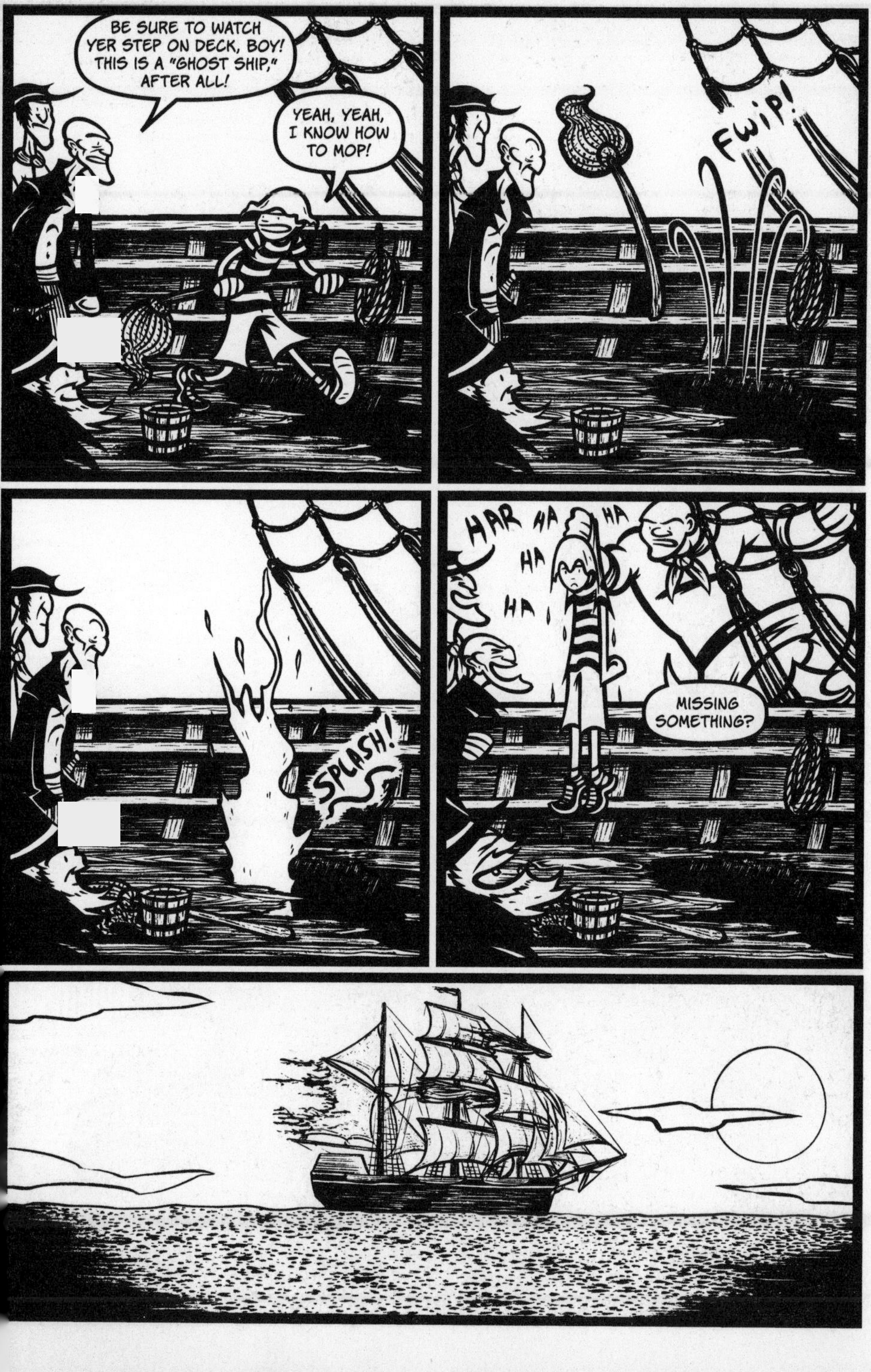
BE SURE TO WATCH YER STEP ON DECK, BOY! THIS IS A "GHOST SHIP," AFTER ALL!
YEAH, YEAH, I KNOW HOW TO MOP!
FWIP!
SPLASH!
HAR HA HA HA HA
MISSING SOMETHING?

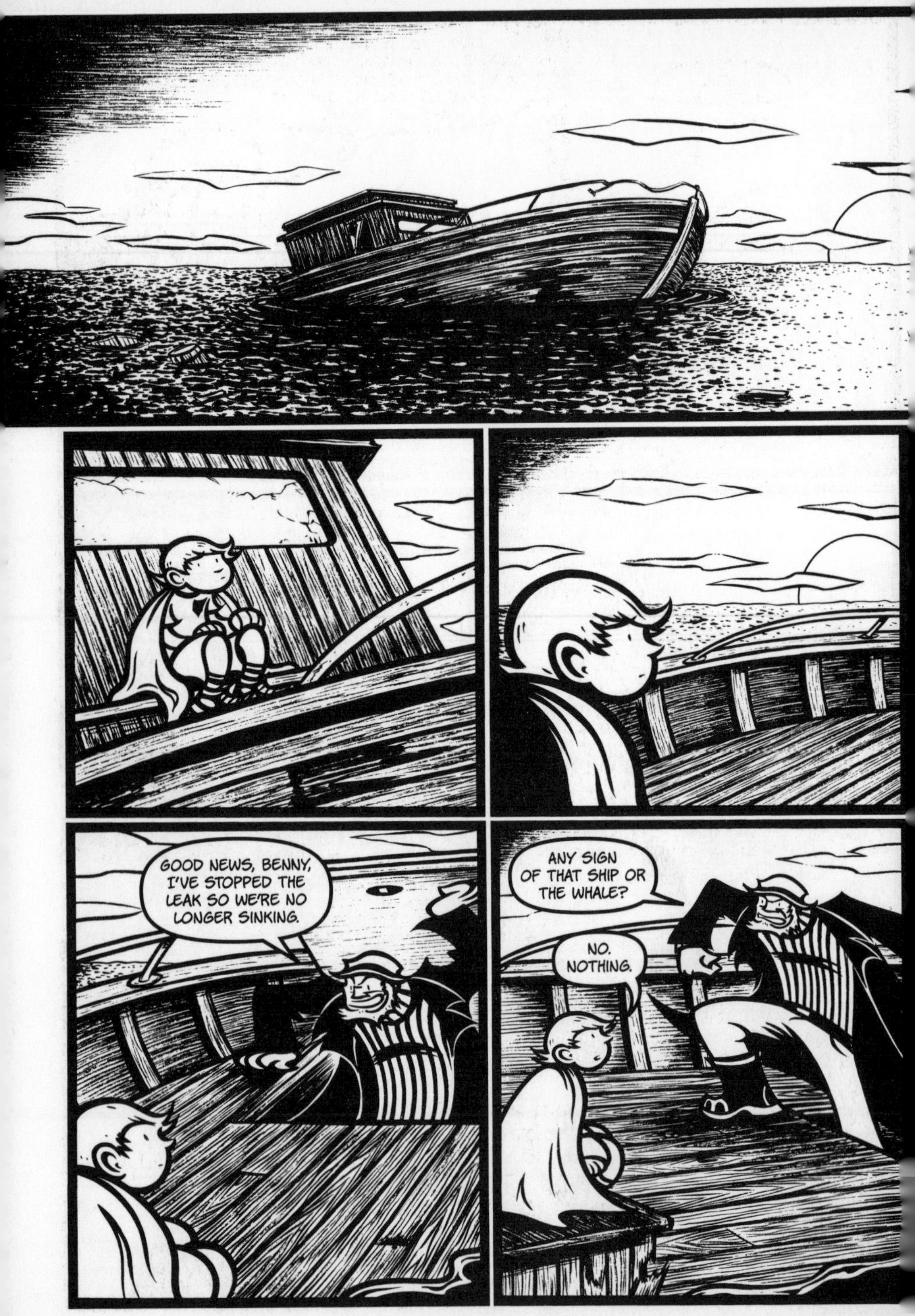
GOOD NEWS, BENNY, I'VE STOPPED THE LEAK SO WE'RE NO LONGER SINKING.
ANY SIGN OF THAT SHIP OR THE WHALE?
NO. NOTHING.

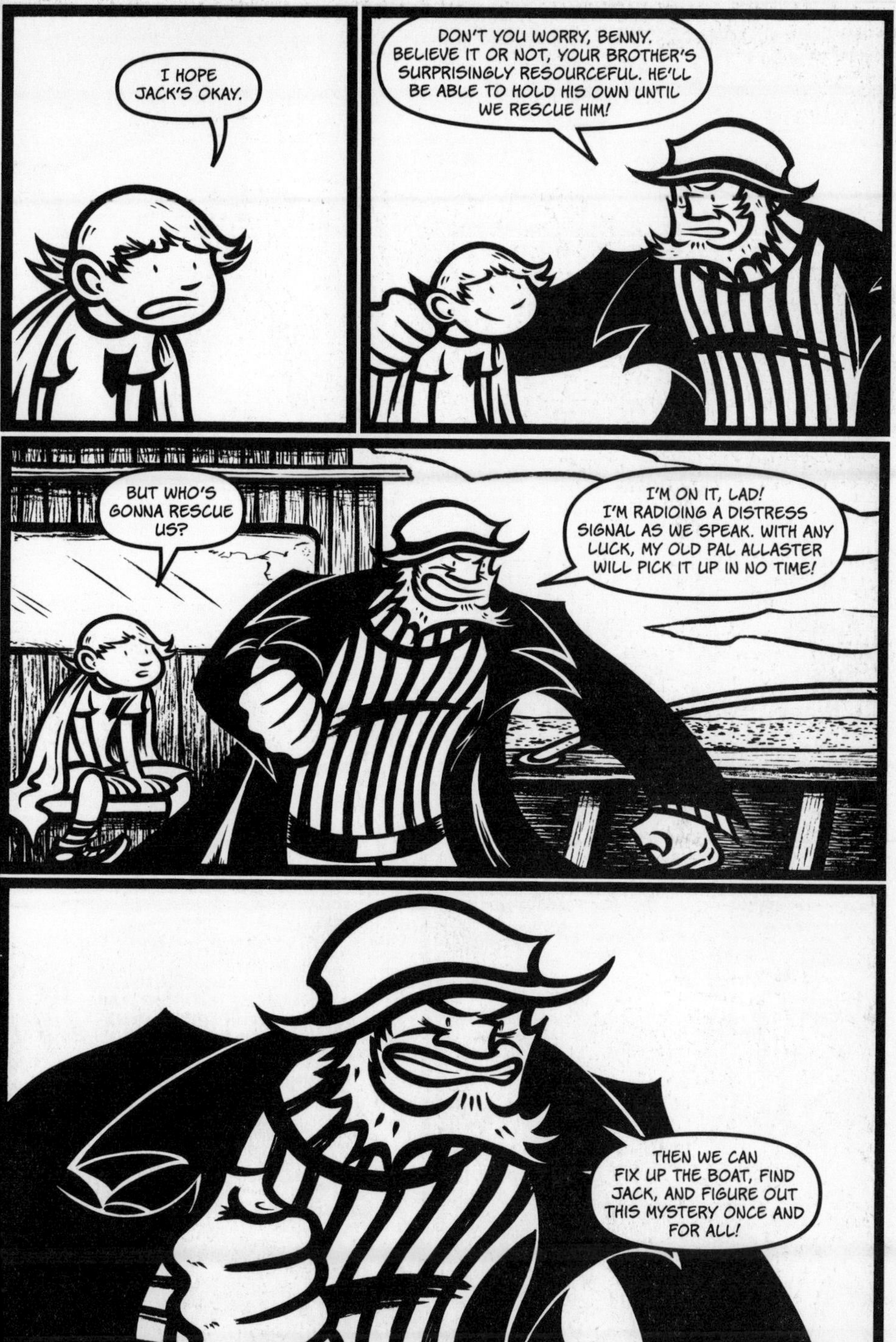
I HOPE JACK'S OKAY.
DON'T YOU WORRY, BENNY. BELIEVE IT OR NOT, YOUR BROTHER'S SURPRISINGLY RESOURCEFUL. HE'LL BE ABLE TO HOLD HIS OWN UNTIL WE RESCUE HIM!
BUT WHO'S GONNA RESCUE US?
I'M ON IT, LAD! I'M RADIOING A DISTRESS SIGNAL AS WE SPEAK. WITH ANY LUCK, MY OLD PAL ALLASTER WILL PICK IT UP IN NO TIME!
THEN WE CAN FIX UP THE BOAT, FIND JACK, AND FIGURE OUT THIS MYSTERY ONCE AND FOR ALL!

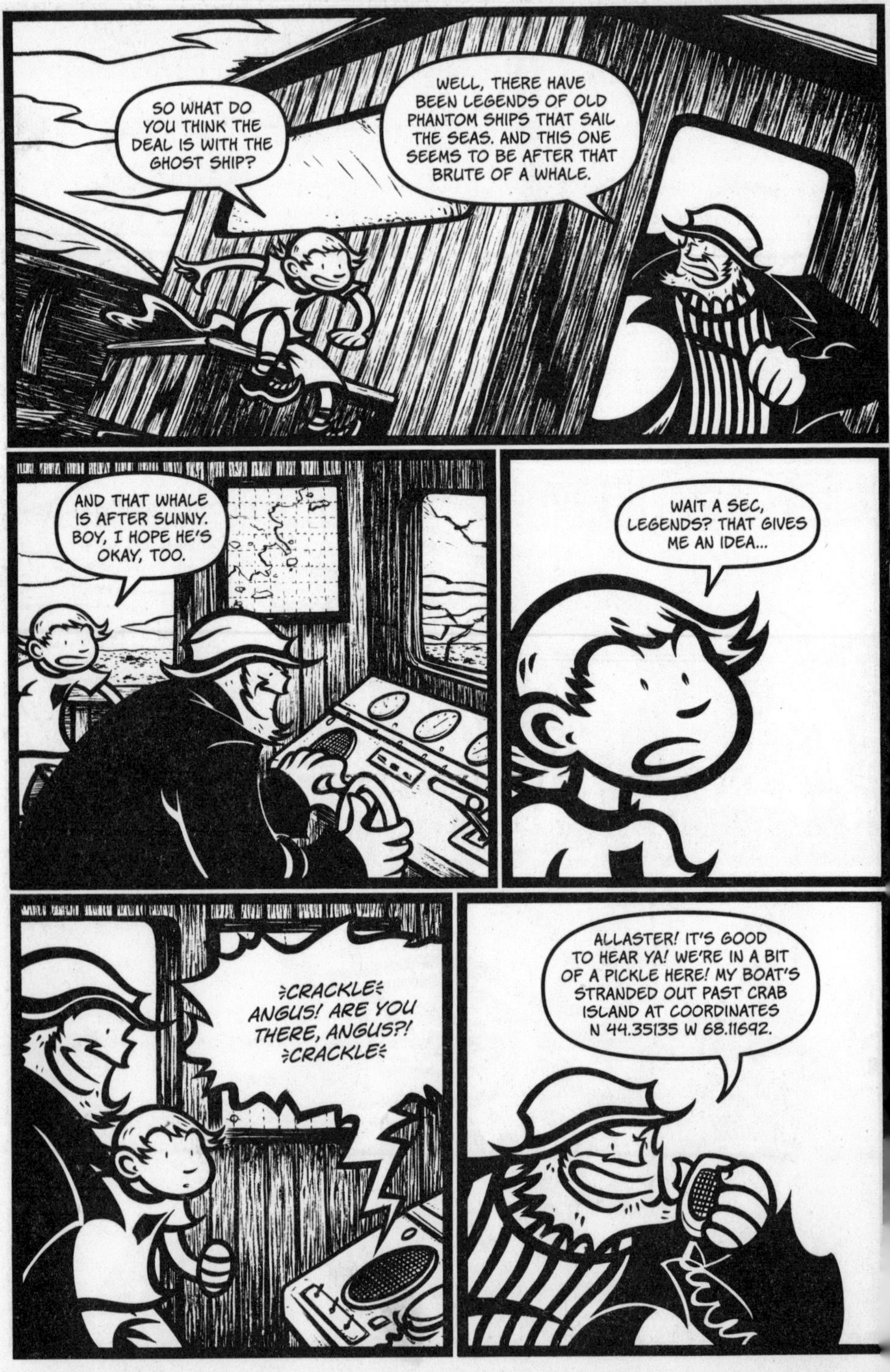
SO WHAT DO YOU THINK THE DEAL IS WITH THE GHOST SHIP?
WELL, THERE HAVE BEEN LEGENDS OF OLD PHANTOM SHIPS THAT SAIL THE SEAS. AND THIS ONE SEEMS TO BE AFTER THAT BRUTE OF A WHALE.
AND THAT WHALE IS AFTER SUNNY. BOY, I HOPE HE'S OKAY, TOO.
WAIT A SEC, LEGENDS? THAT GIVES ME AN IDEA...
CRACKLE ANGUS! ARE YOU THERE, ANGUS?! CRACKLE
ALLASTER! IT'S GOOD TO HEAR YA! WE'RE IN A BIT OF A PICKLE HERE! MY BOAT'S STRANDED OUT PAST CRAB ISLAND AT COORDINATES N 44.35135 W 68.11692.

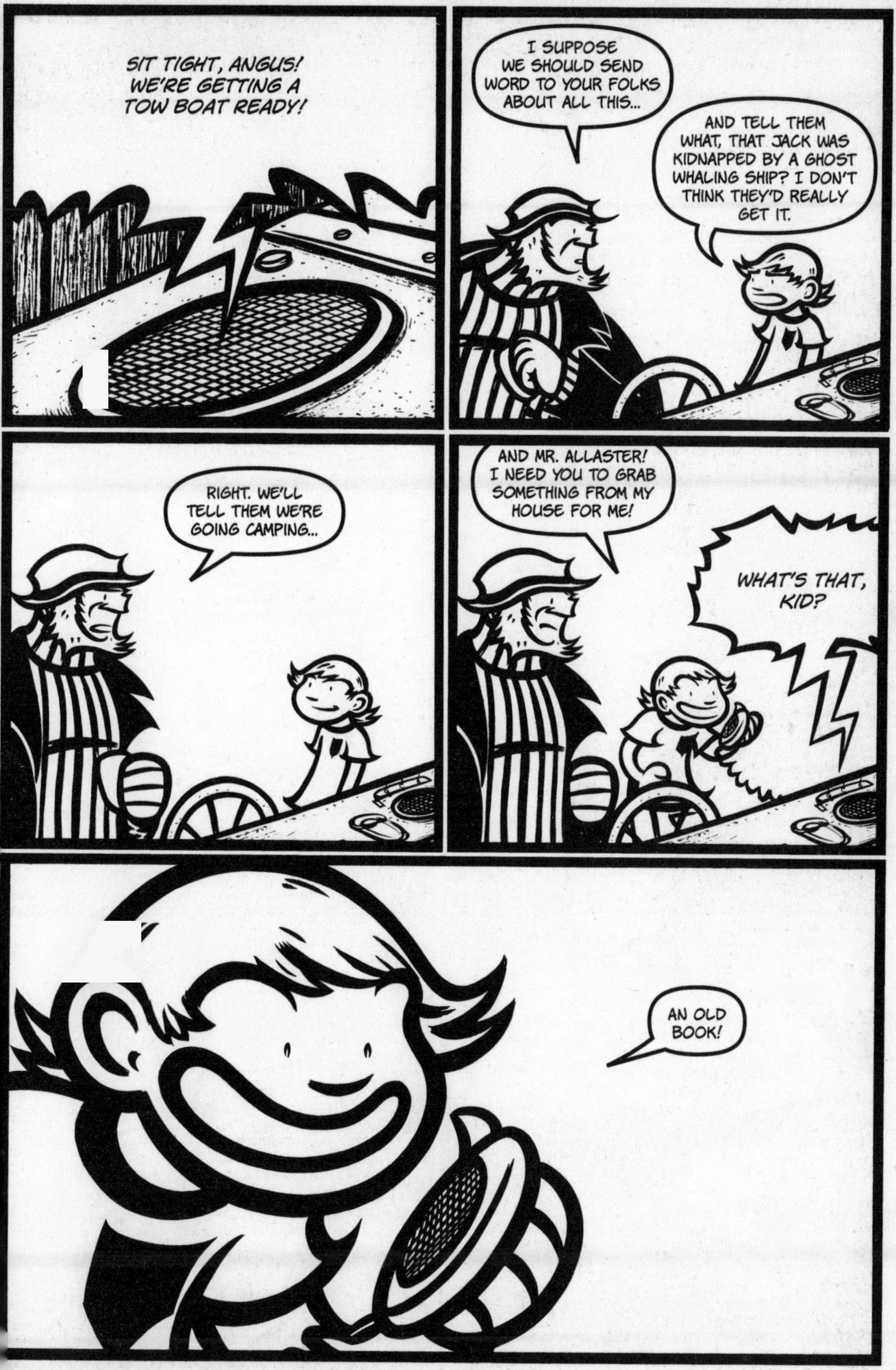
SIT TIGHT, ANGUS! WE'RE GETTING A TOW BOAT READY!
I SUPPOSE WE SHOULD SEND WORD TO YOUR FOLKS ABOUT ALL THIS...
AND TELL THEM WHAT, THAT JACK WAS KIDNAPPED BY A GHOST WHALING SHIP? I DON'T THINK THEY'D REALLY GET IT.
RIGHT. WE'LL TELL THEM WE'RE GOING CAMPING...
AND MR. ALLASTER! I NEED YOU TO GRAB SOMETHING FROM MY HOUSE FOR ME!
WHAT'S THAT, KID?
AN OLD BOOK!

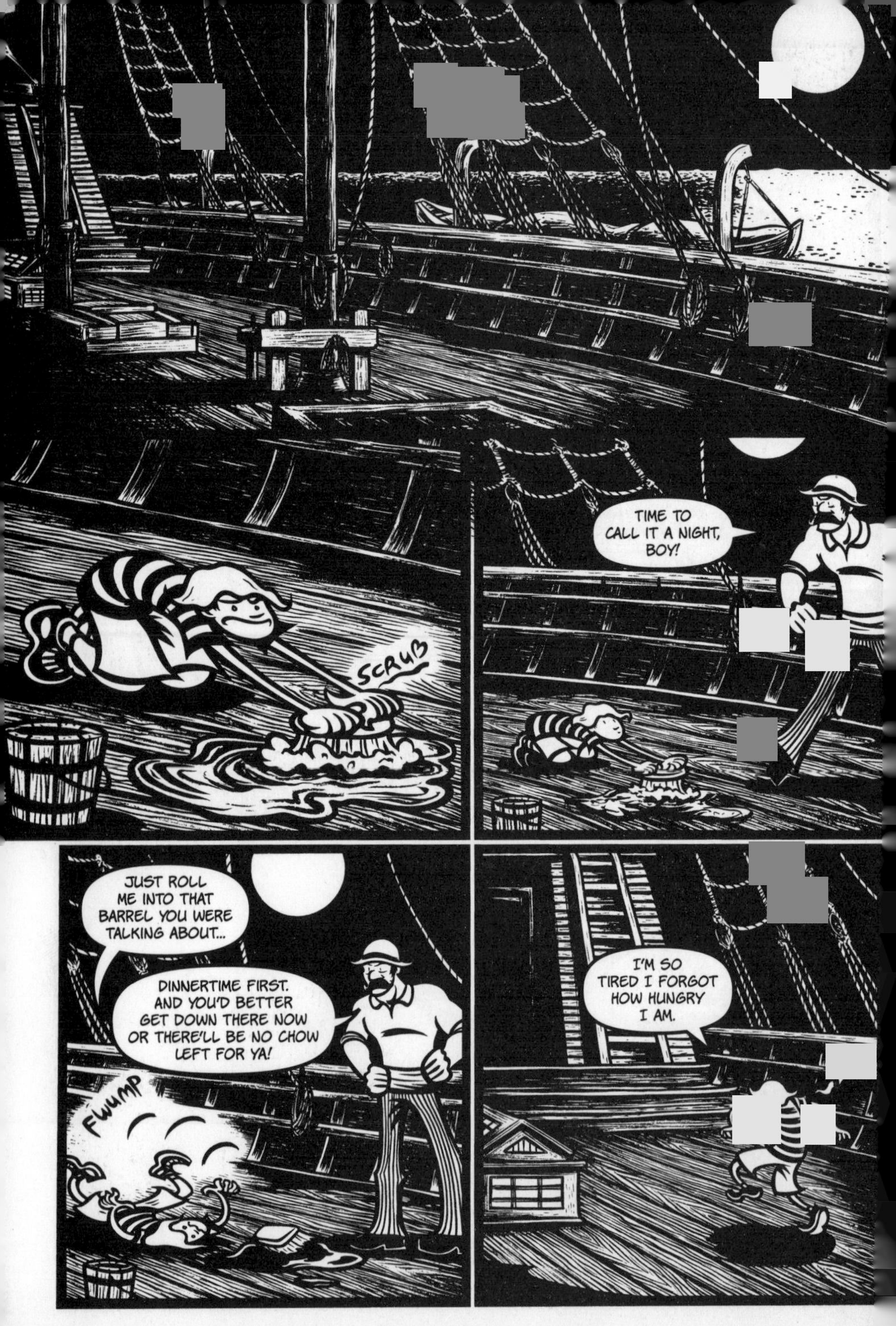
SCRUB
TIME TO CALL IT A NIGHT, BOY!
JUST ROLL ME INTO THAT BARREL YOU WERE TALKING ABOUT...
DINNERTIME FIRST. AND YOU'D BETTER GET DOWN THERE NOW OR THERE'LL BE NO CHOW LEFT FOR YA!
FWUMP
I'M SO TIRED I FORGOT HOW HUNGRY I AM.

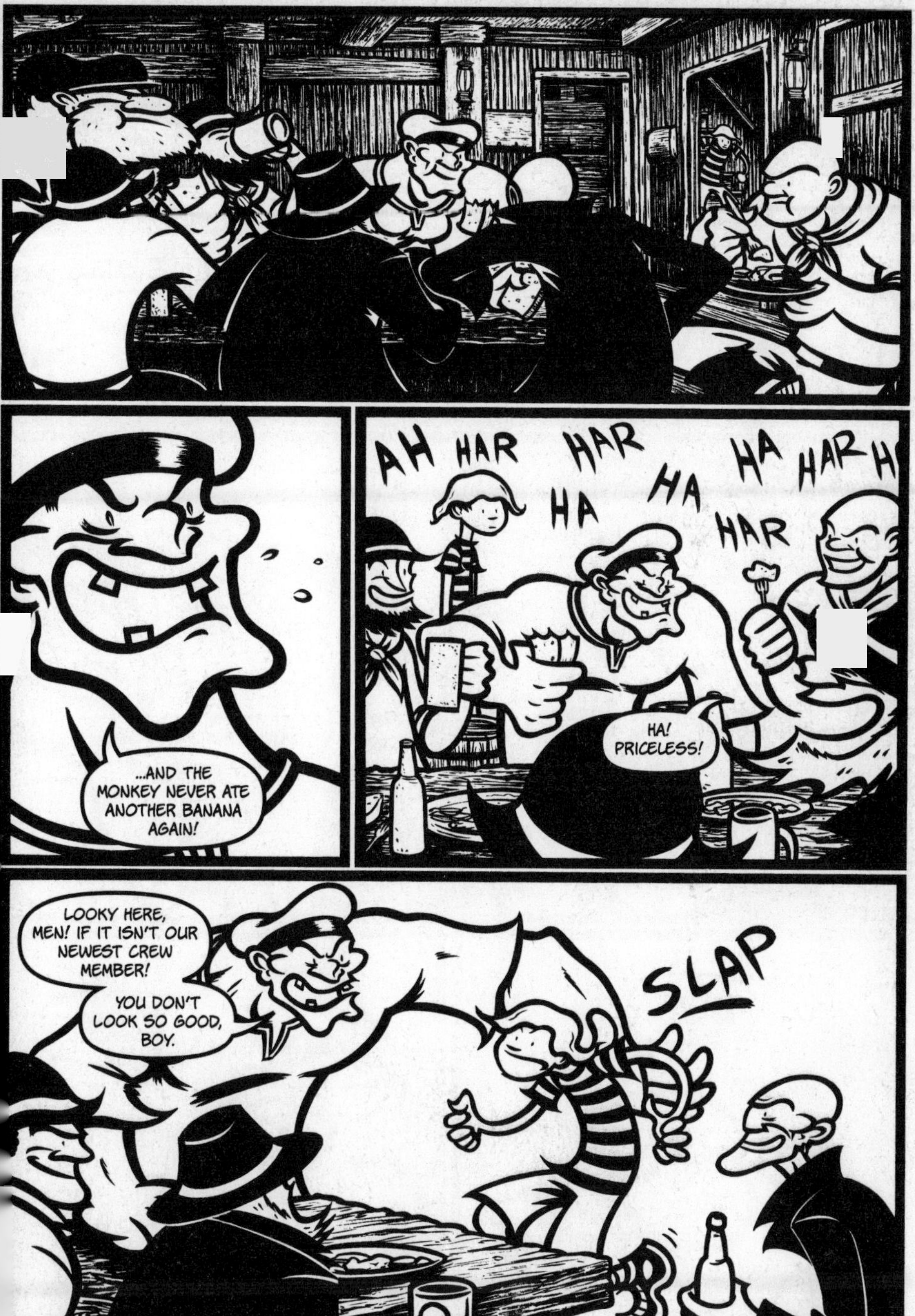
...AND THE MONKEY NEVER ATE ANOTHER BANANA AGAIN!
AH HAR HAR HA HA HA HAR HAR
HA! PRICELESS!
LOOKY HERE, MEN! IF IT ISN'T OUR NEWEST CREW MEMBER!
YOU DON'T LOOK SO GOOD, BOY.
SLAP

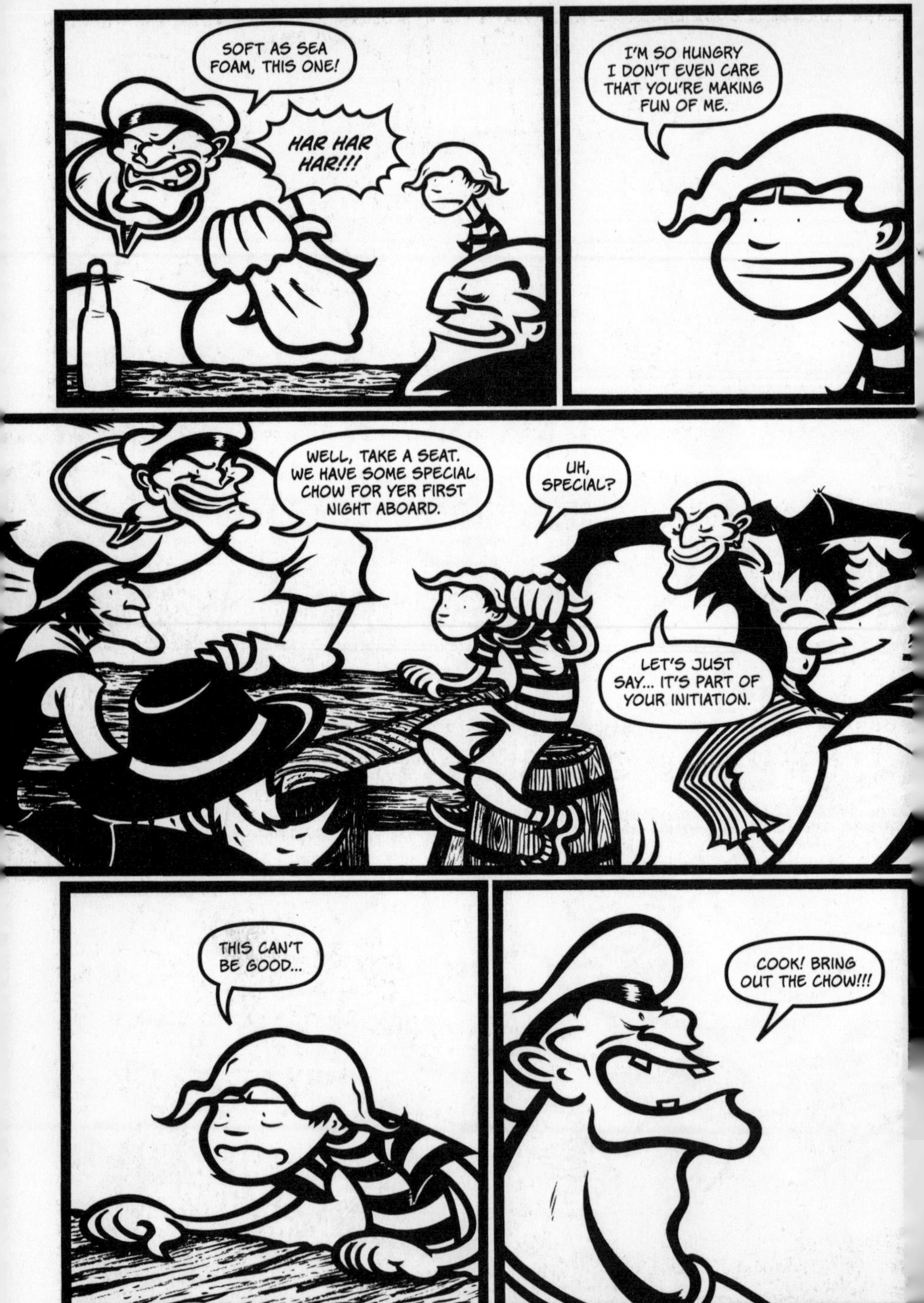
SOFT AS SEA FOAM, THIS ONE!
HAR HAR HAR!!!
I'M SO HUNGRY I DON'T EVEN CARE THAT YOU'RE MAKING FUN OF ME.
WELL, TAKE A SEAT. WE HAVE SOME SPECIAL CHOW FOR YER FIRST NIGHT ABOARD.
UH, SPECIAL?
LET'S JUST SAY... IT'S PART OF YOUR INITIATION.
THIS CAN'T BE GOOD...
COOK! BRING OUT THE CHOW!!!

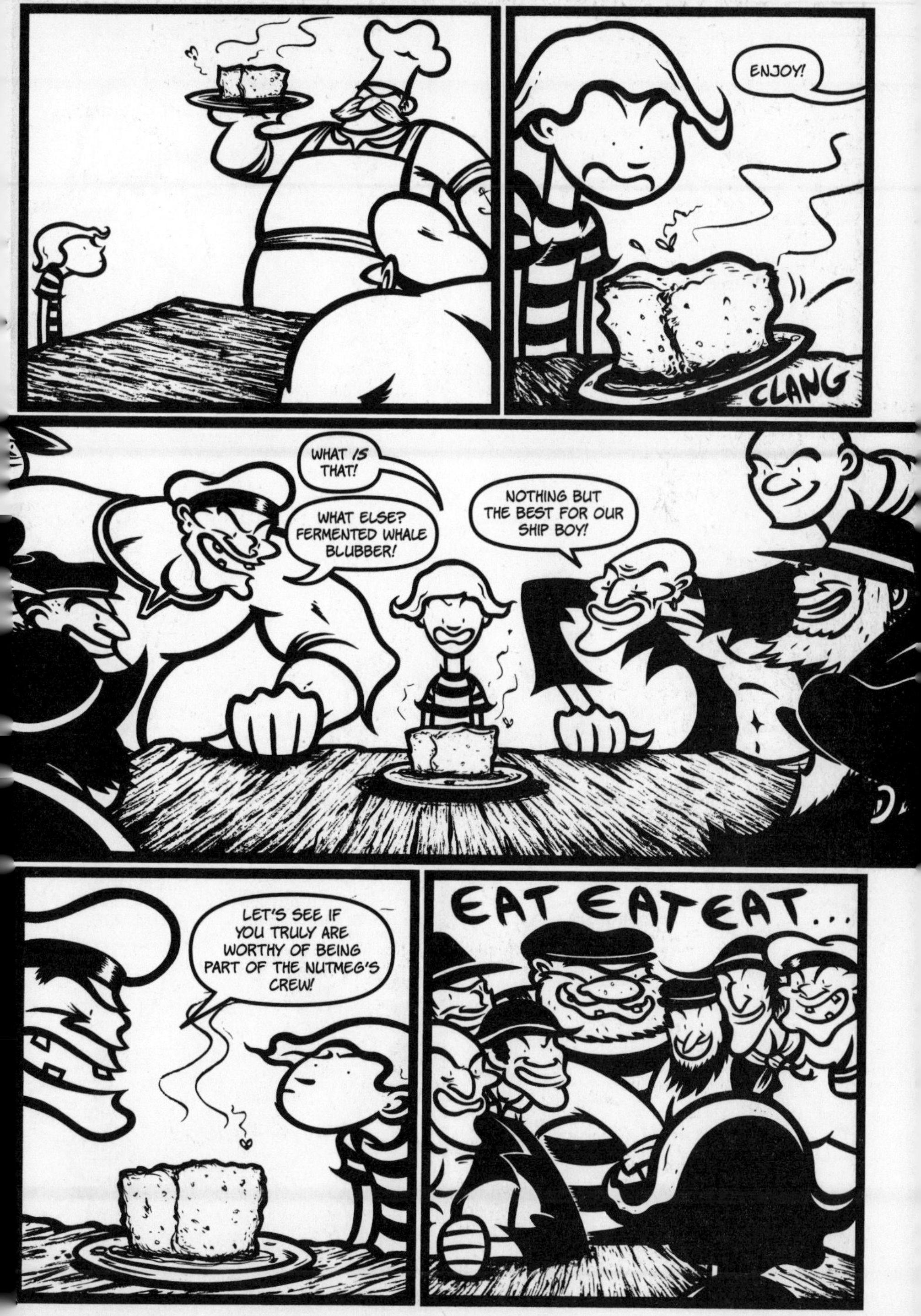
ENJOY!
CLANG
WHAT *IS* THAT!
WHAT ELSE? FERMENTED WHALE BLUBBER!
NOTHING BUT THE BEST FOR OUR SHIP BOY!
LET'S SEE IF YOU TRULY ARE WORTHY OF BEING PART OF THE NUTMEG'S CREW!
EAT EAT EAT EAT...

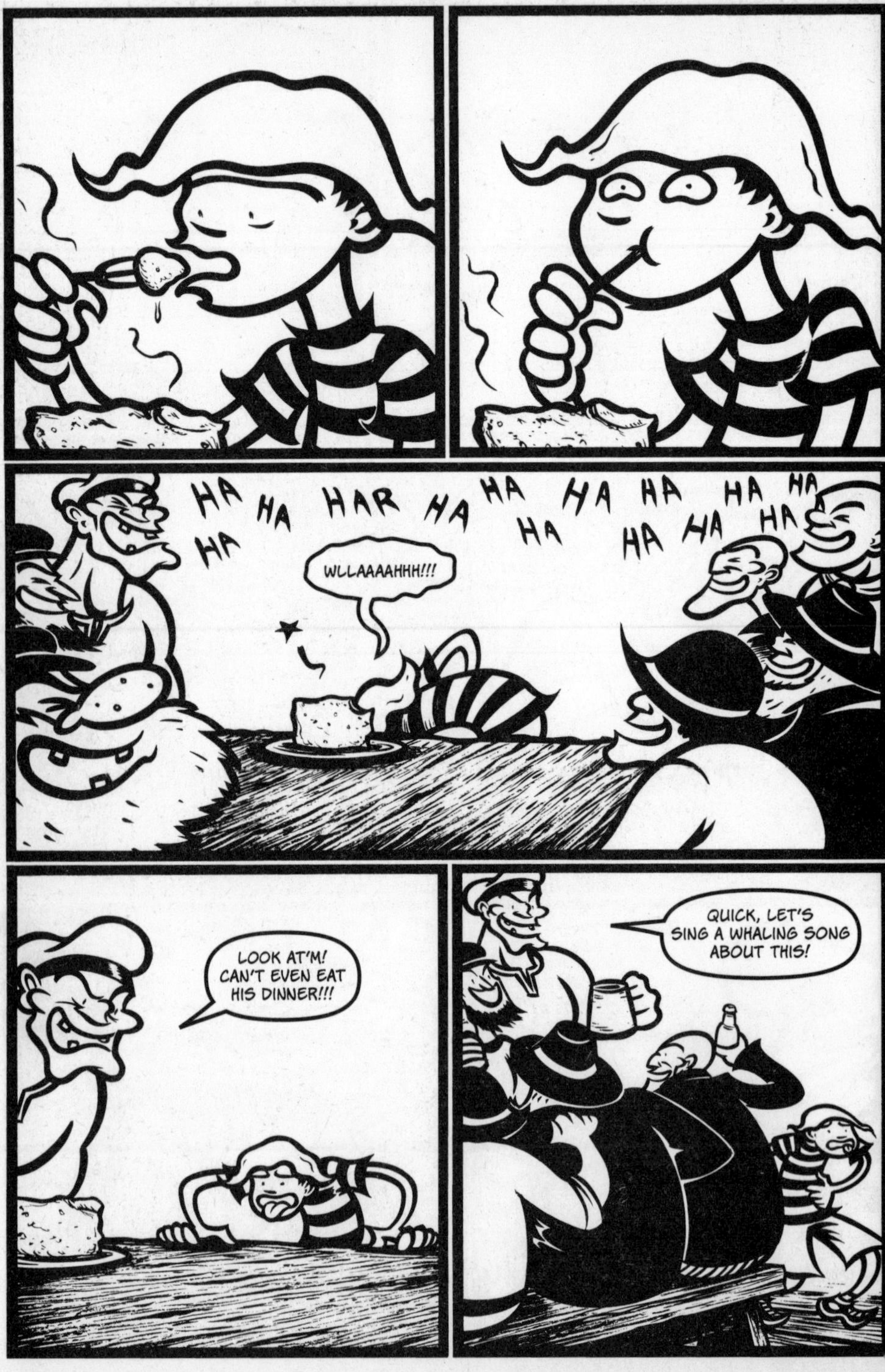
HA HA HAR HA HA HA HA HA HA HA HA HA HA HA
WLLAAAAHHH!!!
LOOK AT'M! CAN'T EVEN EAT HIS DINNER!!!
QUICK, LET'S SING A WHALING SONG ABOUT THIS!

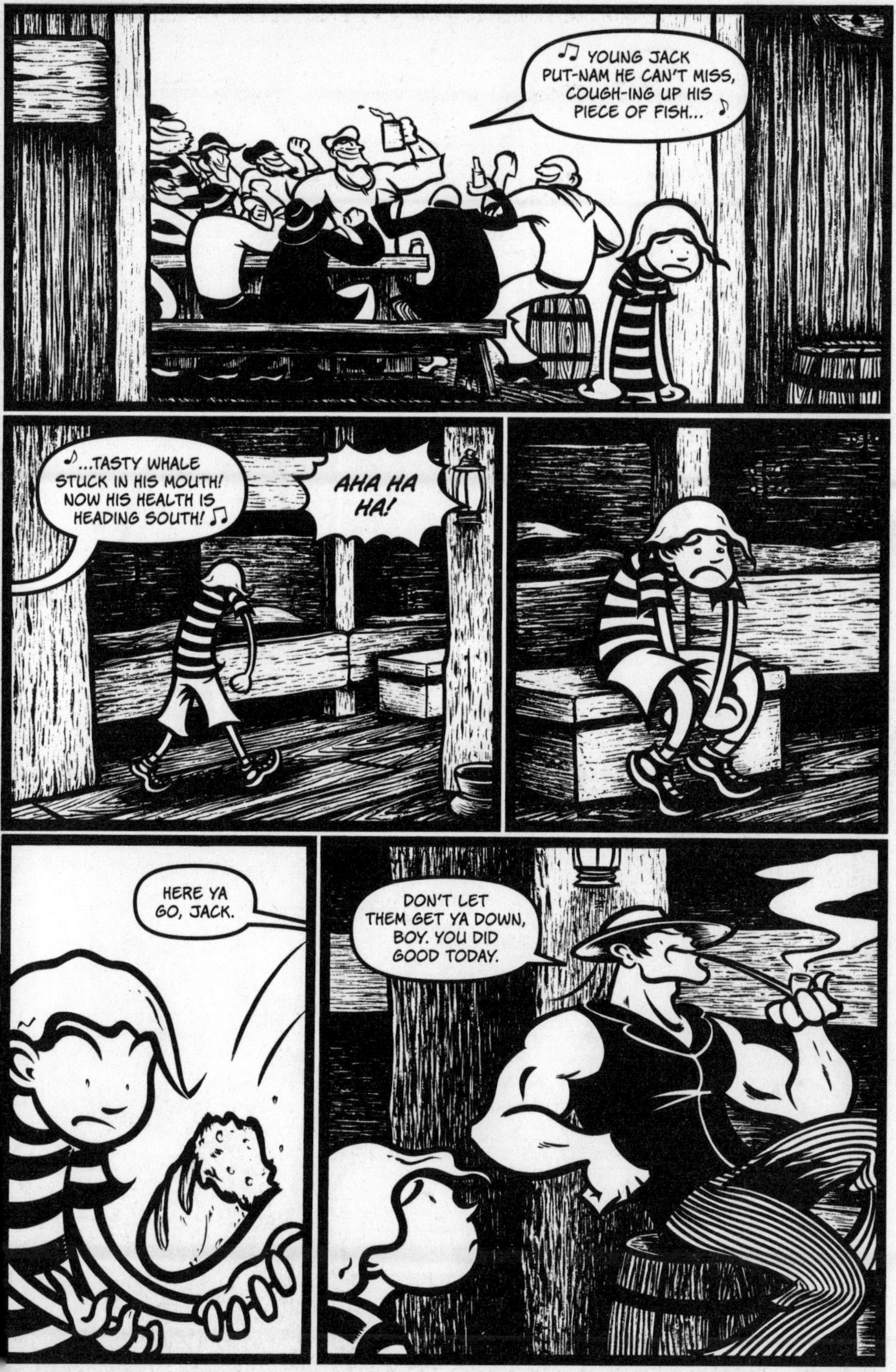
♫ YOUNG JACK PUT-NAM HE CAN'T MISS, COUGH-ING UP HIS PIECE OF FISH... ♪
♪ ...TASTY WHALE STUCK IN HIS MOUTH! NOW HIS HEALTH IS HEADING SOUTH! ♫
AHA HA HA!
HERE YA GO, JACK.
DON'T LET THEM GET YA DOWN, BOY. YOU DID GOOD TODAY.

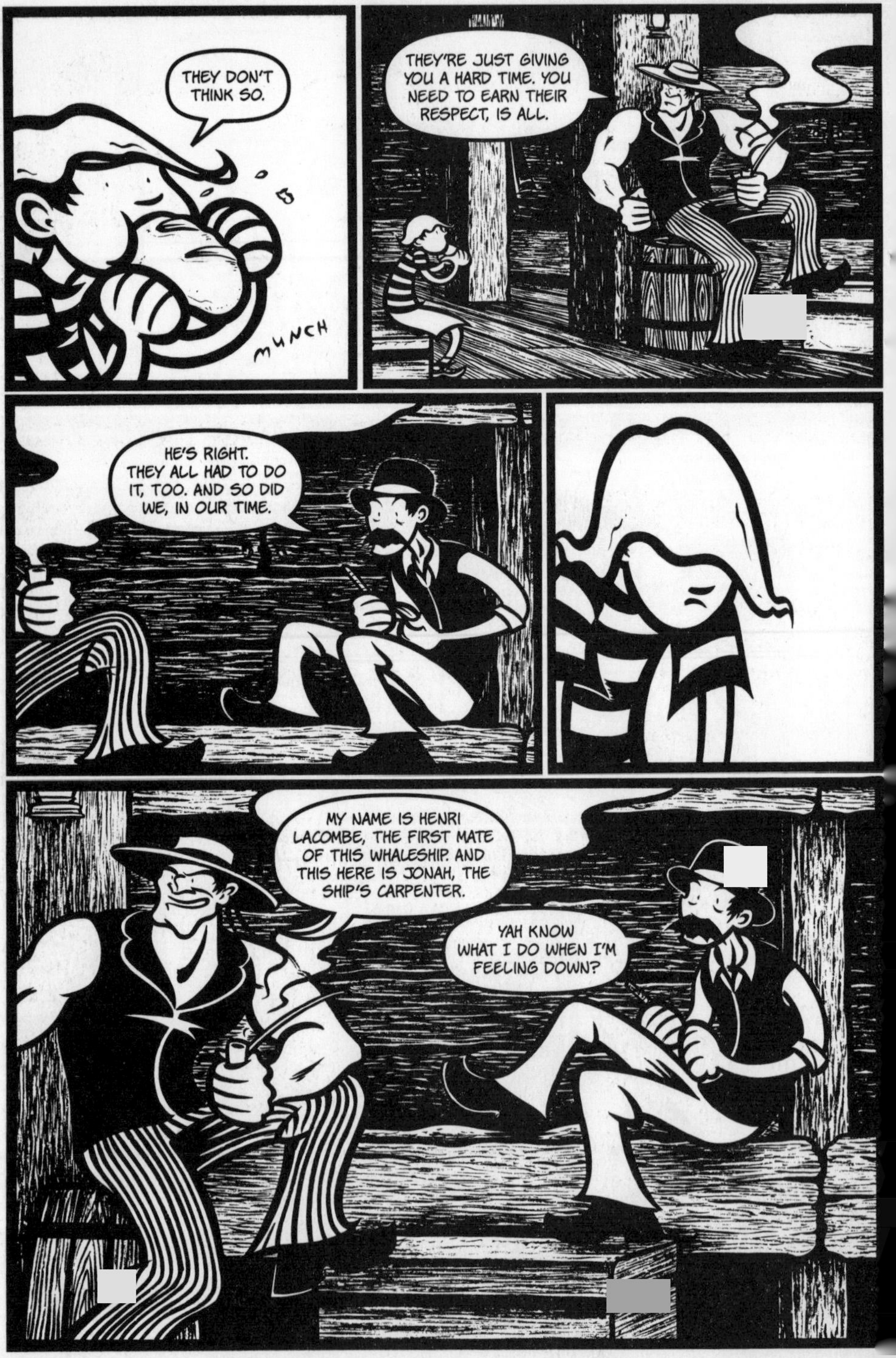
THEY DON'T THINK SO.
MUNCH
THEY'RE JUST GIVING YOU A HARD TIME. YOU NEED TO EARN THEIR RESPECT, IS ALL.
HE'S RIGHT. THEY ALL HAD TO DO IT, TOO. AND SO DID WE, IN OUR TIME.
MY NAME IS HENRI LACOMBE, THE FIRST MATE OF THIS WHALESHIP. AND THIS HERE IS JONAH, THE SHIP'S CARPENTER.
YAH KNOW WHAT I DO WHEN I'M FEELING DOWN?

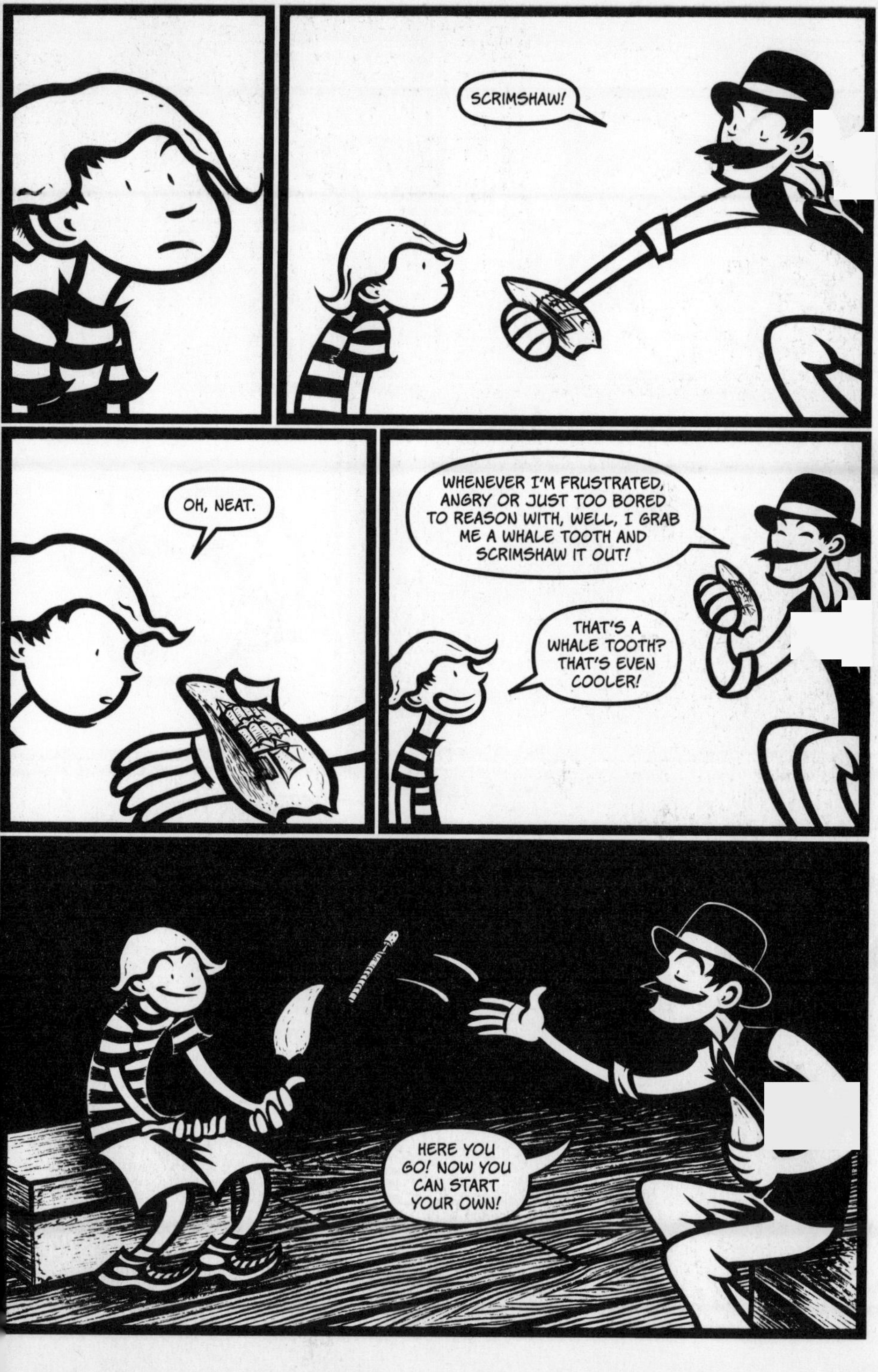
SCRIMSHAW!
OH, NEAT.
WHENEVER I'M FRUSTRATED, ANGRY OR JUST TOO BORED TO REASON WITH, WELL, I GRAB ME A WHALE TOOTH AND SCRIMSHAW IT OUT!
THAT'S A WHALE TOOTH? THAT'S EVEN COOLER!
HERE YOU GO! NOW YOU CAN START YOUR OWN!

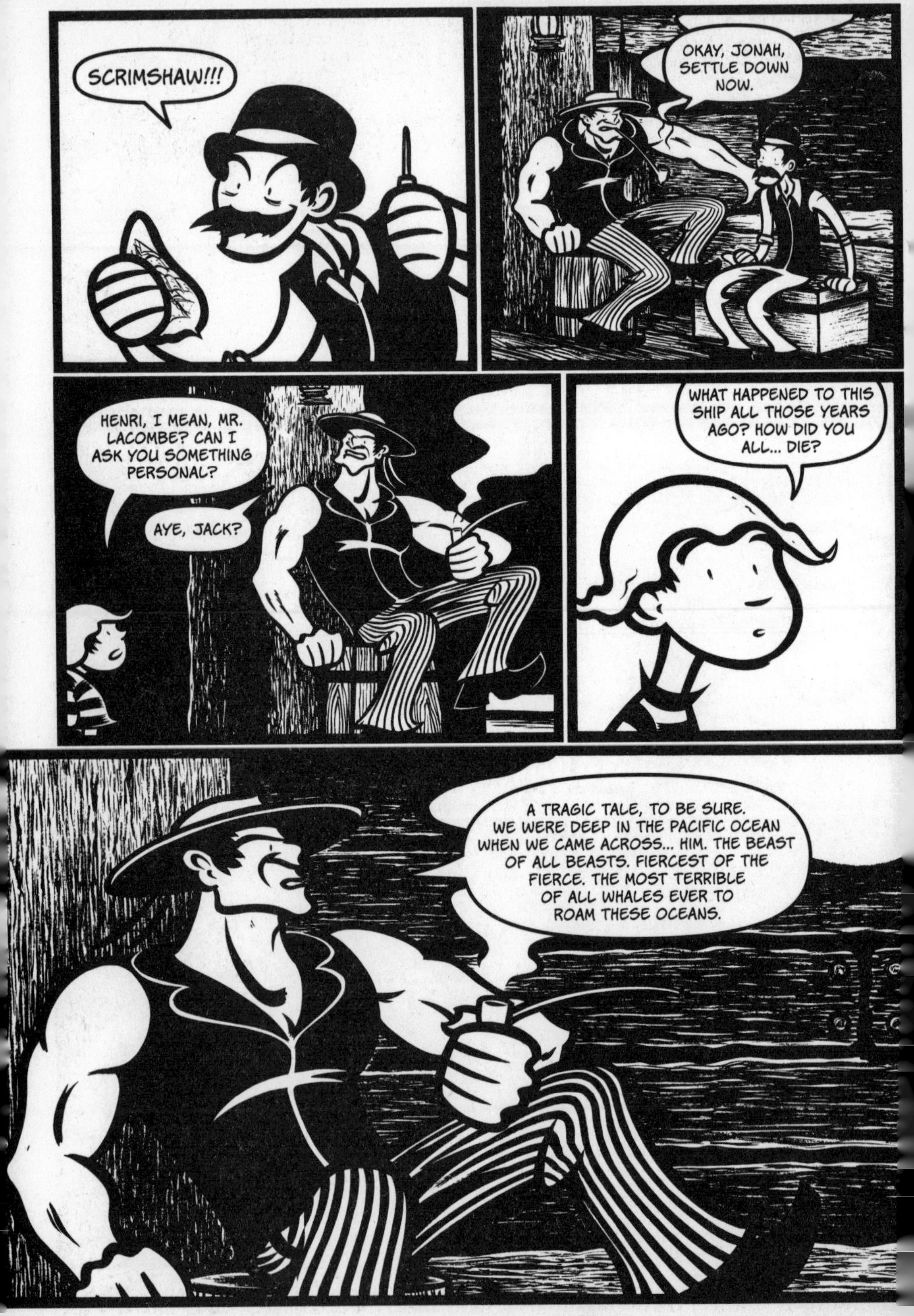
SCRIMSHAW!!!
OKAY, JONAH, SETTLE DOWN NOW.
HENRI, I MEAN, MR. LACOMBE? CAN I ASK YOU SOMETHING PERSONAL?
AYE, JACK?
WHAT HAPPENED TO THIS SHIP ALL THOSE YEARS AGO? HOW DID YOU ALL... DIE?
A TRAGIC TALE, TO BE SURE. WE WERE DEEP IN THE PACIFIC OCEAN WHEN WE CAME ACROSS... HIM. THE BEAST OF ALL BEASTS. FIERCEST OF THE FIERCE. THE MOST TERRIBLE OF ALL WHALES EVER TO ROAM THESE OCEANS.

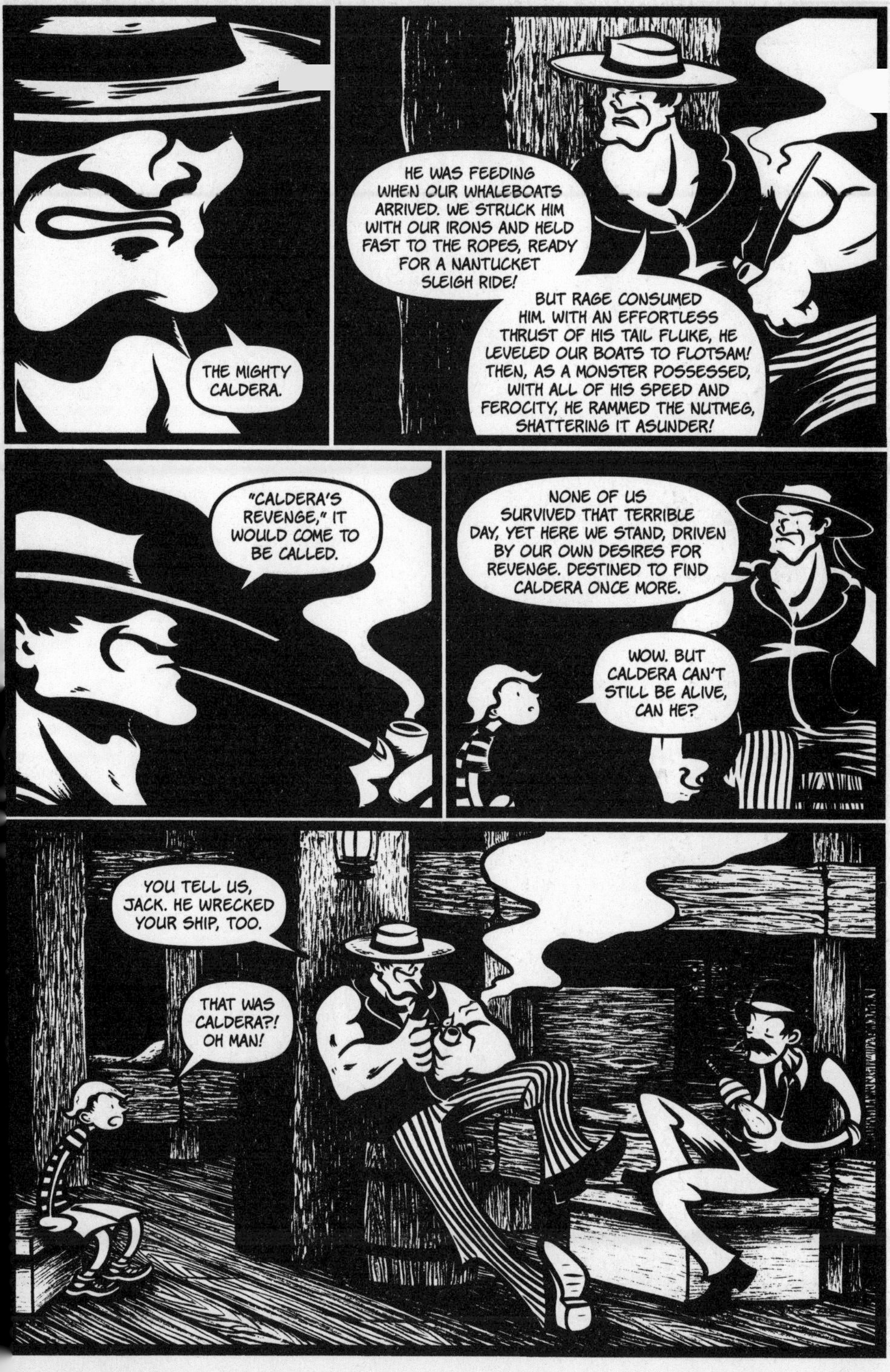
THE MIGHTY CALDERA.
HE WAS FEEDING WHEN OUR WHALEBOATS ARRIVED. WE STRUCK HIM WITH OUR IRONS AND HELD FAST TO THE ROPES, READY FOR A NANTUCKET SLEIGH RIDE!
BUT RAGE CONSUMED HIM. WITH AN EFFORTLESS THRUST OF HIS TAIL FLUKE, HE LEVELED OUR BOATS TO FLOTSAM! THEN, AS A MONSTER POSSESSED, WITH ALL OF HIS SPEED AND FEROCITY, HE RAMMED THE NUTMEG, SHATTERING IT ASUNDER!
"CALDERA'S REVENGE," IT WOULD COME TO BE CALLED.
NONE OF US SURVIVED THAT TERRIBLE DAY, YET HERE WE STAND, DRIVEN BY OUR OWN DESIRES FOR REVENGE. DESTINED TO FIND CALDERA ONCE MORE.
WOW. BUT CALDERA CAN'T STILL BE ALIVE, CAN HE?
YOU TELL US, JACK. HE WRECKED YOUR SHIP, TOO.
THAT WAS CALDERA?! OH MAN!

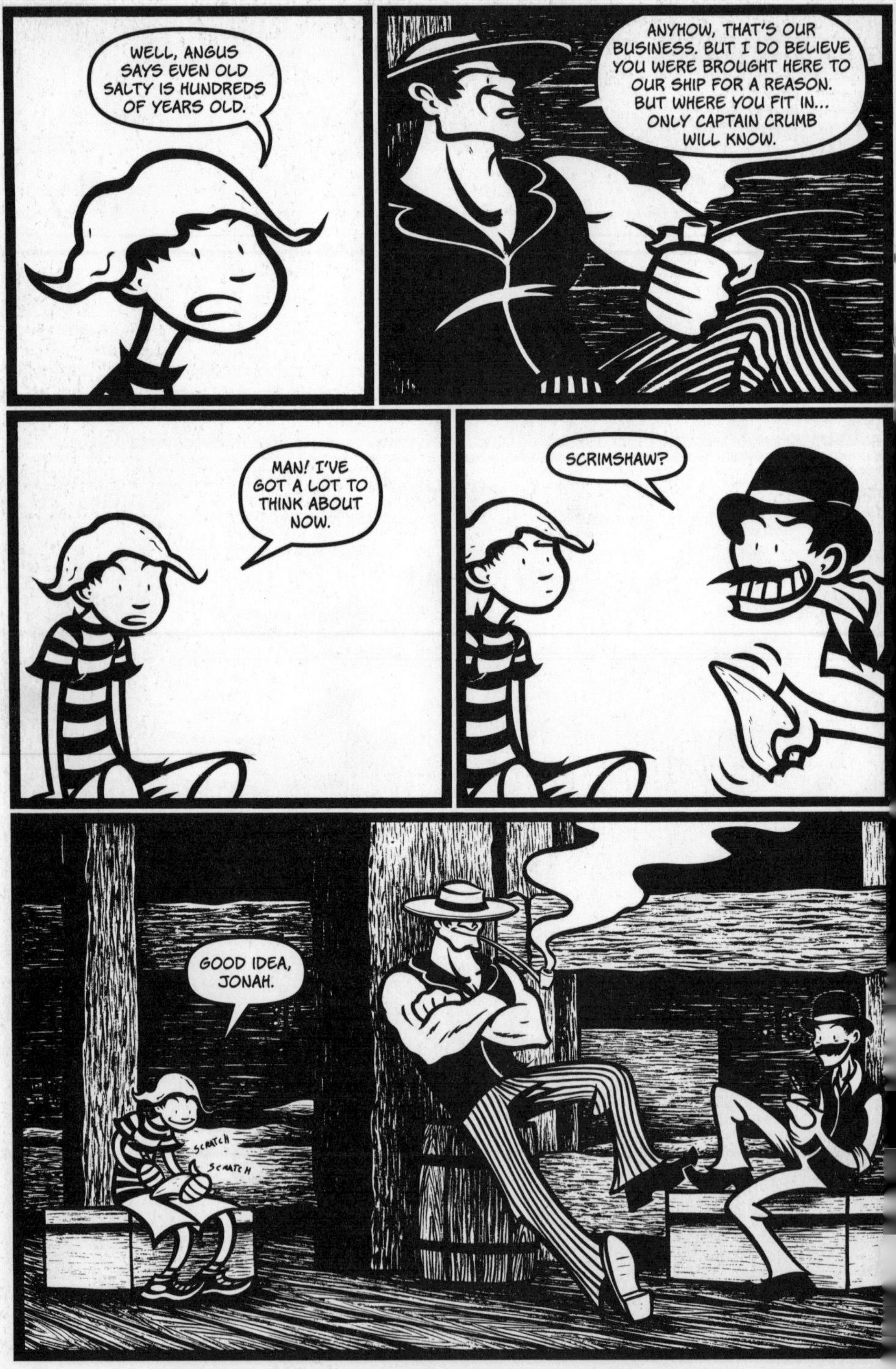
WELL, ANGUS SAYS EVEN OLD SALTY IS HUNDREDS OF YEARS OLD.
ANYHOW, THAT'S OUR BUSINESS. BUT I DO BELIEVE YOU WERE BROUGHT HERE TO OUR SHIP FOR A REASON. BUT WHERE YOU FIT IN... ONLY CAPTAIN CRUMB WILL KNOW.
MAN! I'VE GOT A LOT TO THINK ABOUT NOW.
SCRIMSHAW?
GOOD IDEA, JONAH.
SCRATCH
SCRATCH

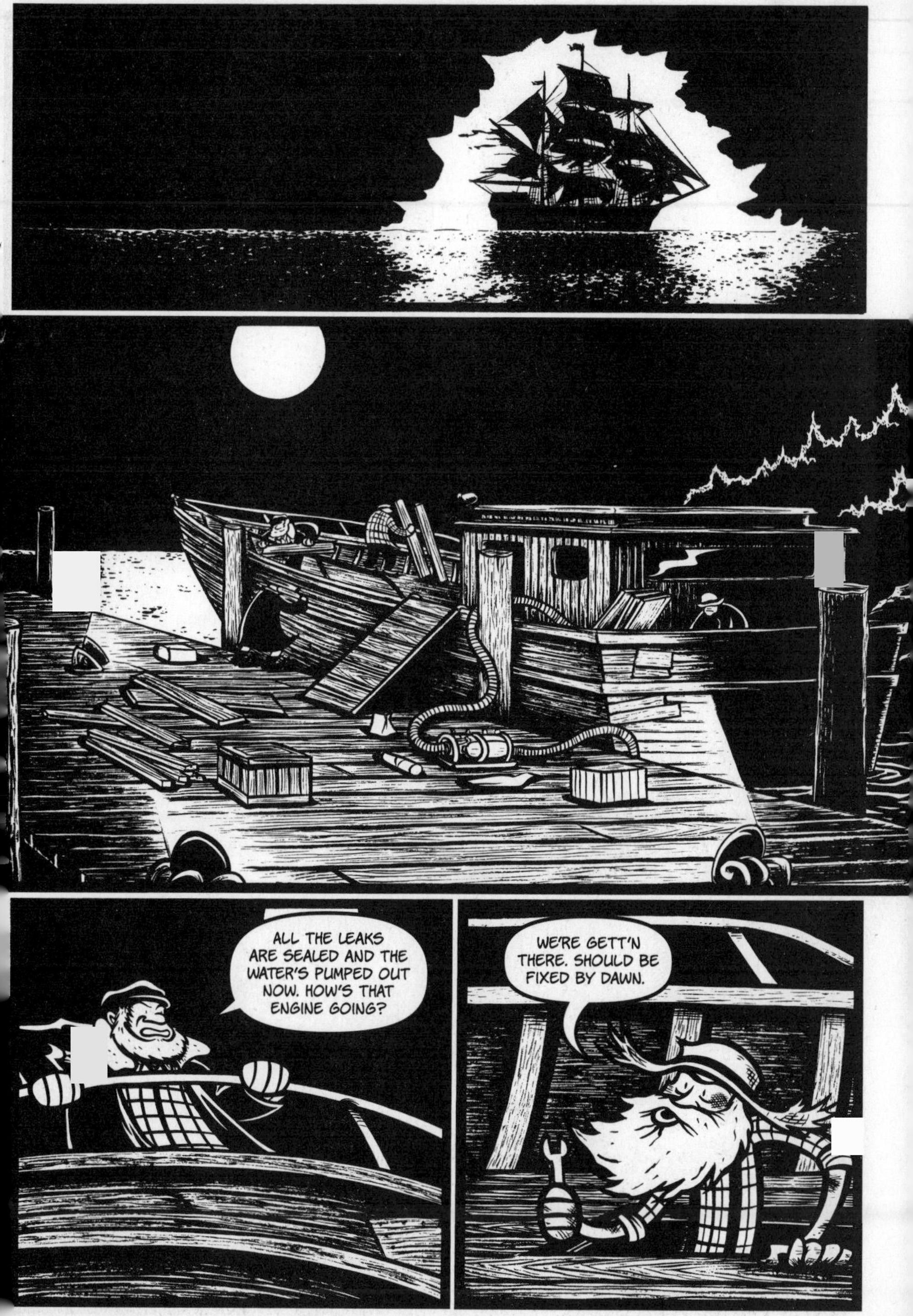
ALL THE LEAKS ARE SEALED AND THE WATER'S PUMPED OUT NOW. HOW'S THAT ENGINE GOING?
WE'RE GETT'N THERE. SHOULD BE FIXED BY DAWN.

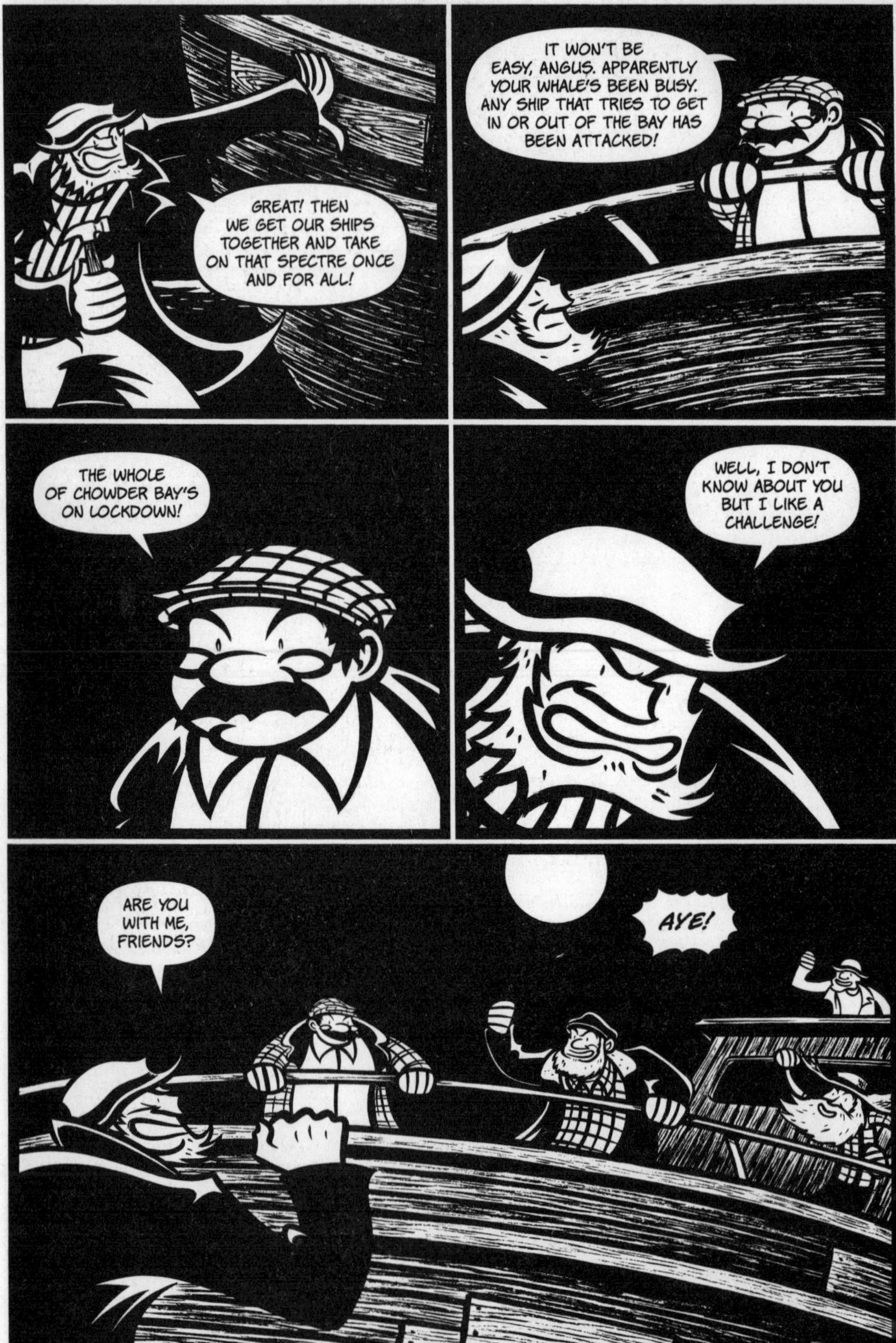
GREAT! THEN WE GET OUR SHIPS TOGETHER AND TAKE ON THAT SPECTRE ONCE AND FOR ALL!
IT WON'T BE EASY, ANGUS. APPARENTLY YOUR WHALE'S BEEN BUSY. ANY SHIP THAT TRIES TO GET IN OR OUT OF THE BAY HAS BEEN ATTACKED!
THE WHOLE OF CHOWDER BAY'S ON LOCKDOWN!
WELL, I DON'T KNOW ABOUT YOU BUT I LIKE A CHALLENGE!
ARE YOU WITH ME, FRIENDS?
AYE!

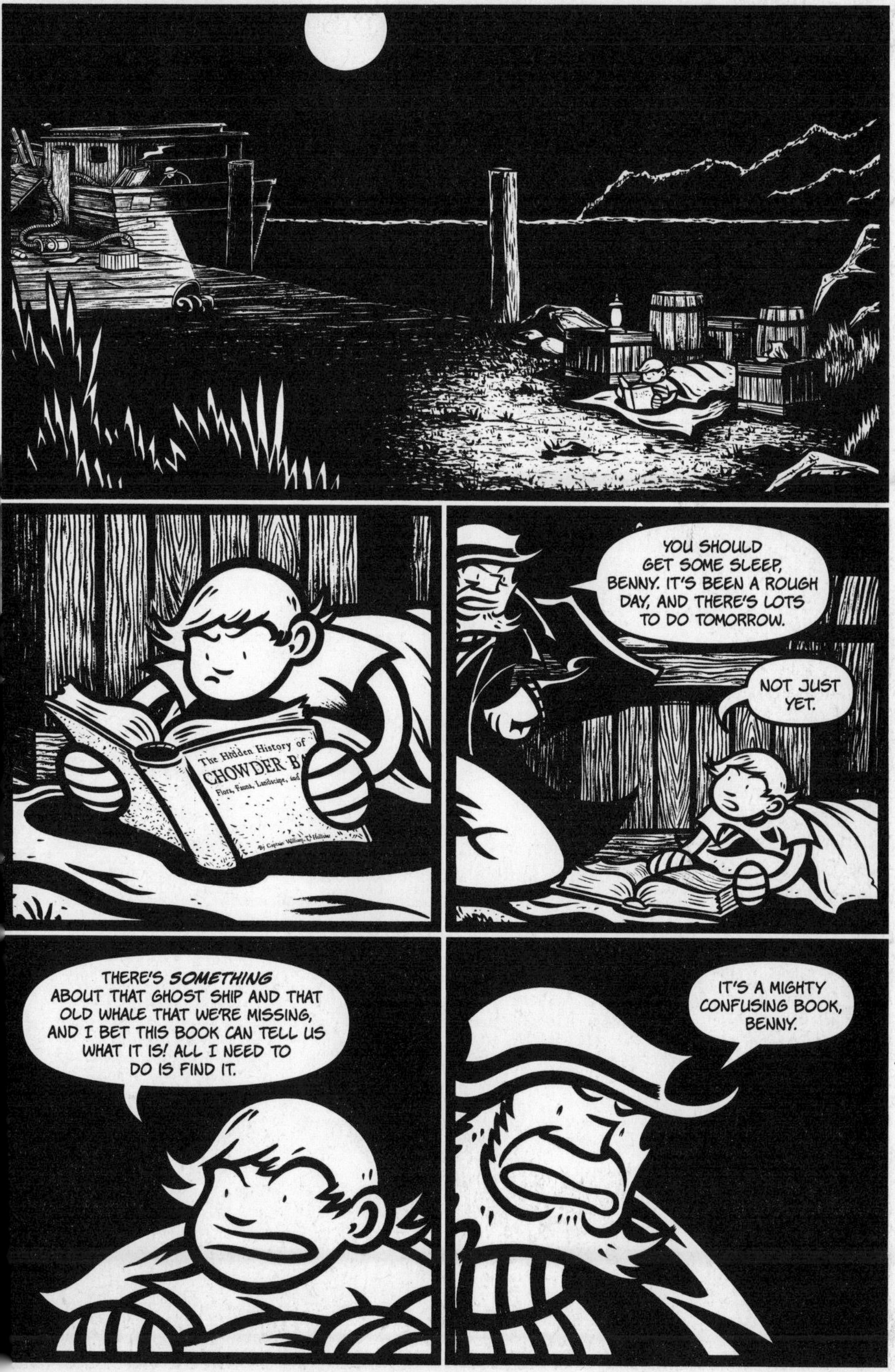
The Hidden History of
CHOWDER BA
Flora, Fauna, Landscape, and
YOU SHOULD GET SOME SLEEP, BENNY. IT'S BEEN A ROUGH DAY, AND THERE'S LOTS TO DO TOMORROW.
NOT JUST YET.
THERE'S *SOMETHING* ABOUT THAT GHOST SHIP AND THAT OLD WHALE THAT WE'RE MISSING, AND I BET THIS BOOK CAN TELL US WHAT IT IS! ALL I NEED TO DO IS FIND IT.
IT'S A MIGHTY CONFUSING BOOK, BENNY.

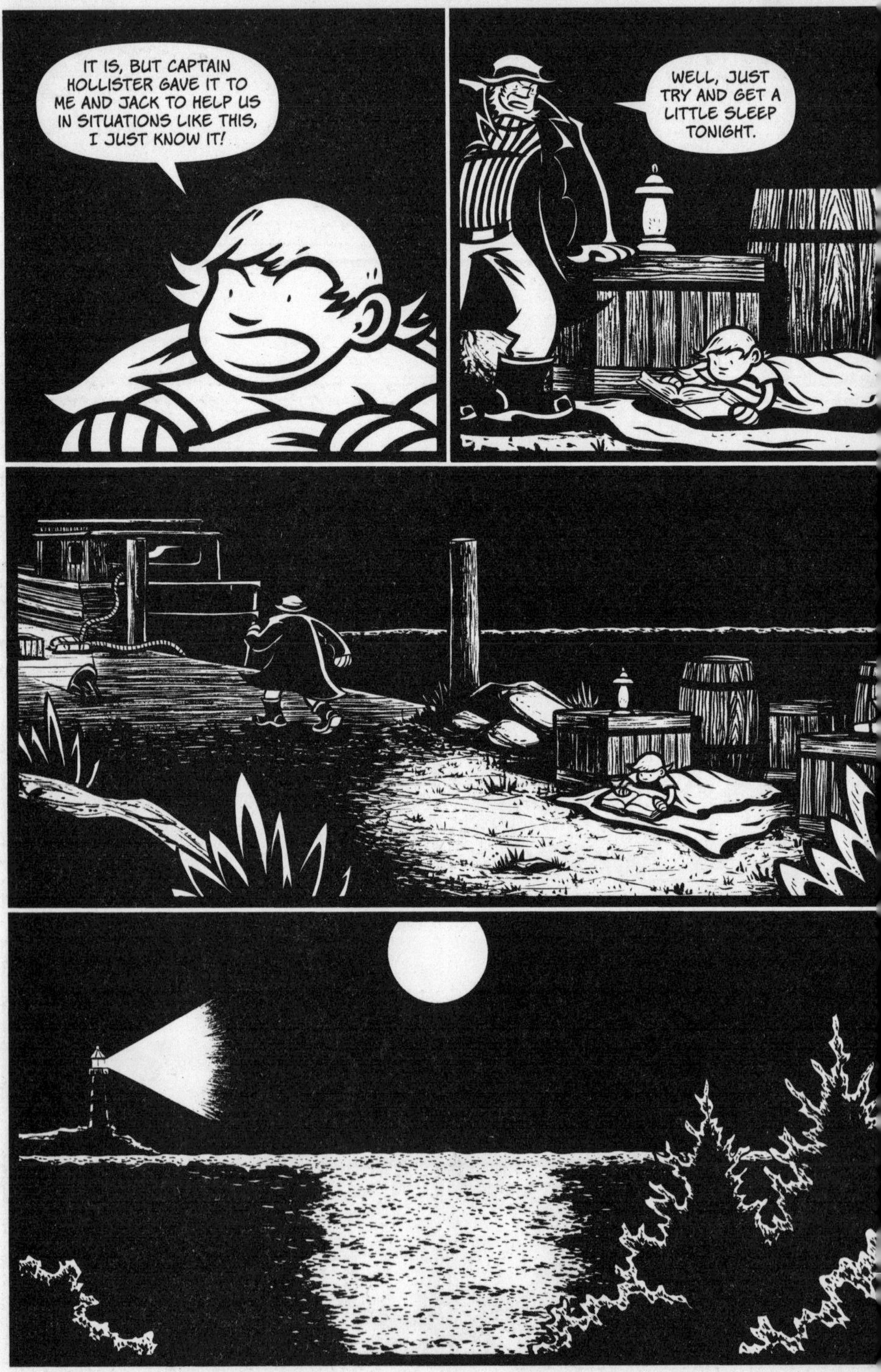
IT IS, BUT CAPTAIN HOLLISTER GAVE IT TO ME AND JACK TO HELP US IN SITUATIONS LIKE THIS, I JUST KNOW IT!
WELL, JUST TRY AND GET A LITTLE SLEEP TONIGHT.

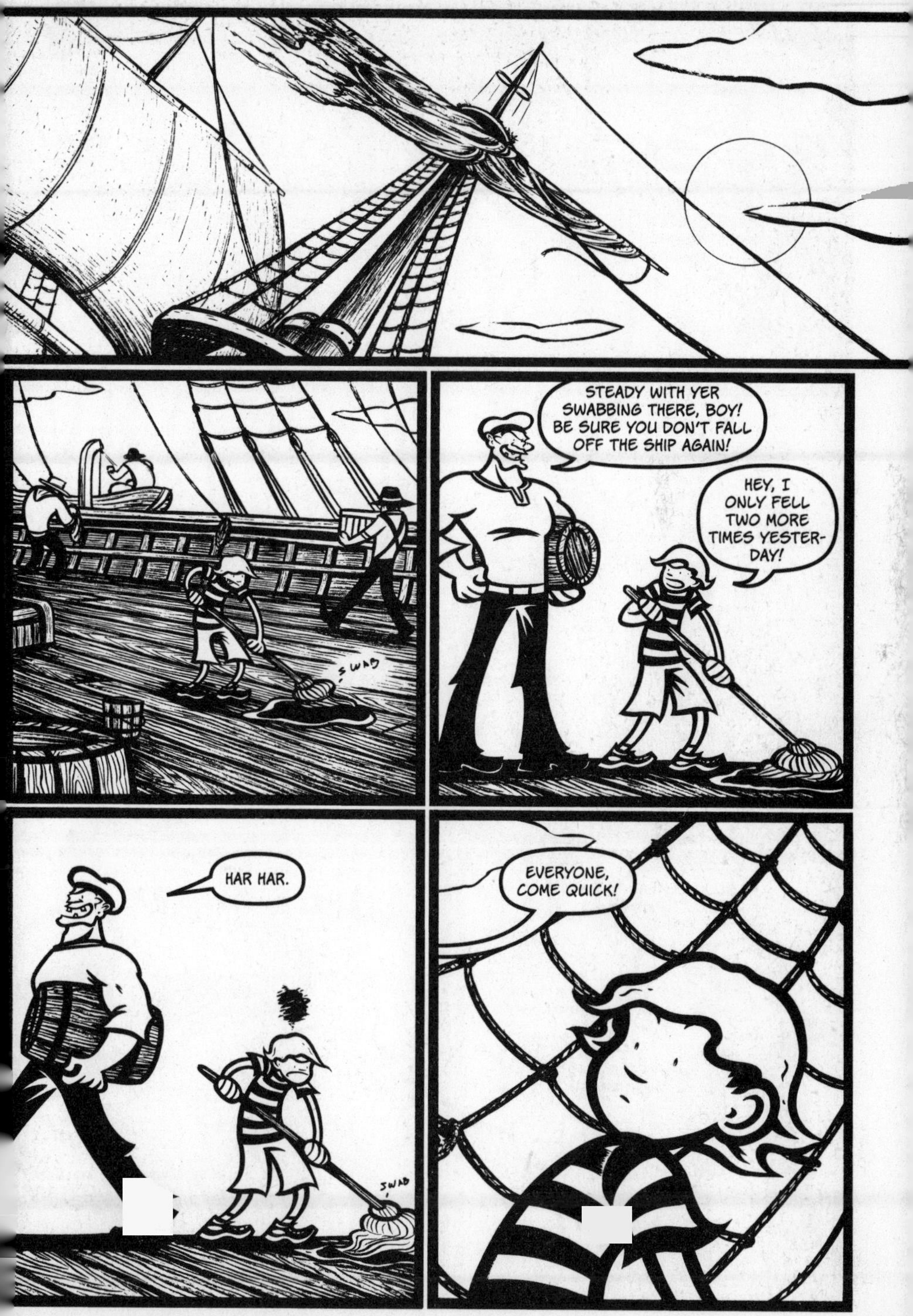
SWAB
STEADY WITH YER SWABBING THERE, BOY! BE SURE YOU DON'T FALL OFF THE SHIP AGAIN!
HEY, I ONLY FELL TWO MORE TIMES YESTER-DAY!
HAR HAR.
SWAB
EVERYONE, COME QUICK!

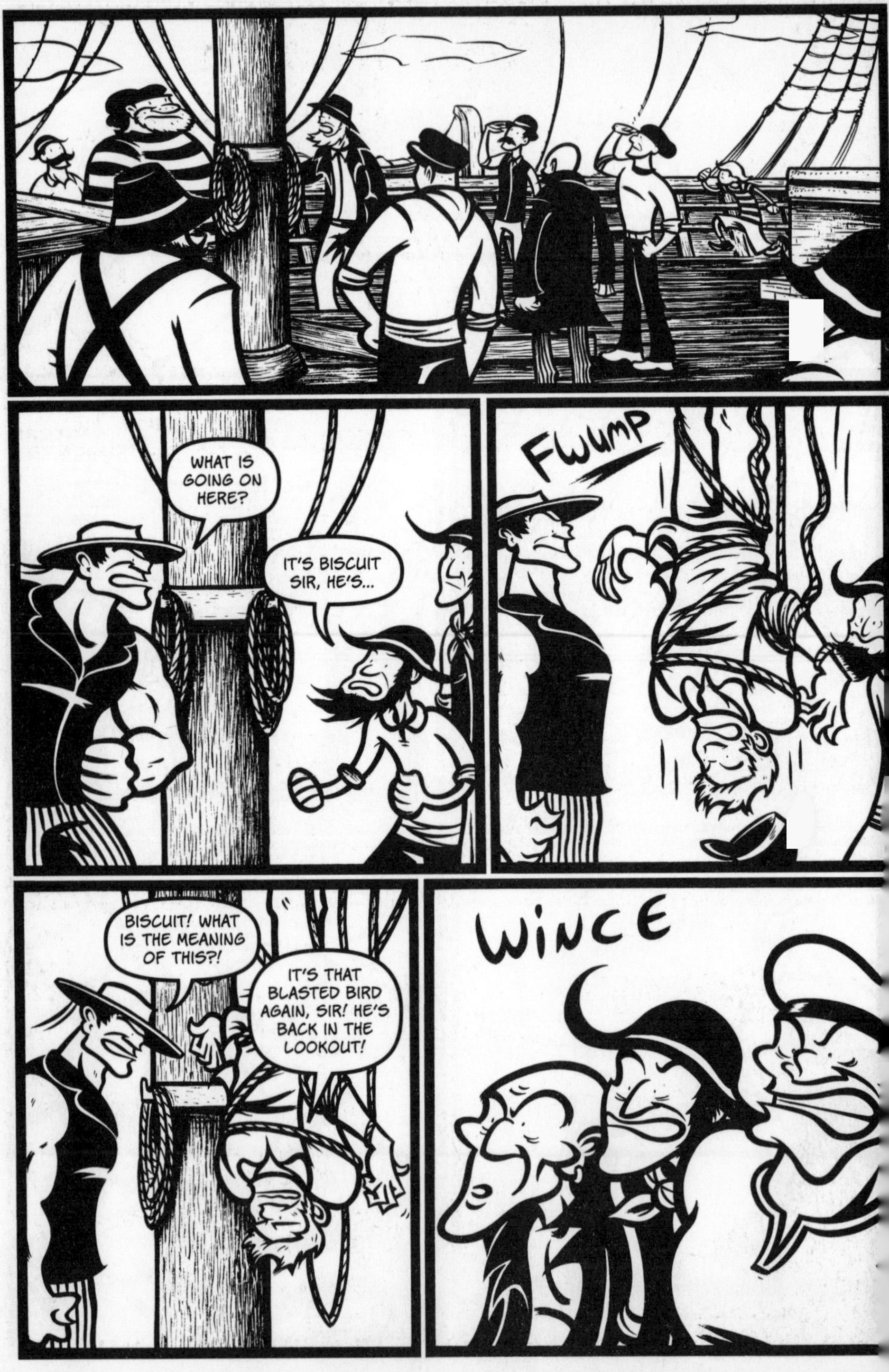
WHAT IS GOING ON HERE?
IT'S BISCUIT SIR, HE'S...
FWUMP
BISCUIT! WHAT IS THE MEANING OF THIS?!
IT'S THAT BLASTED BIRD AGAIN, SIR! HE'S BACK IN THE LOOKOUT!
WINCE

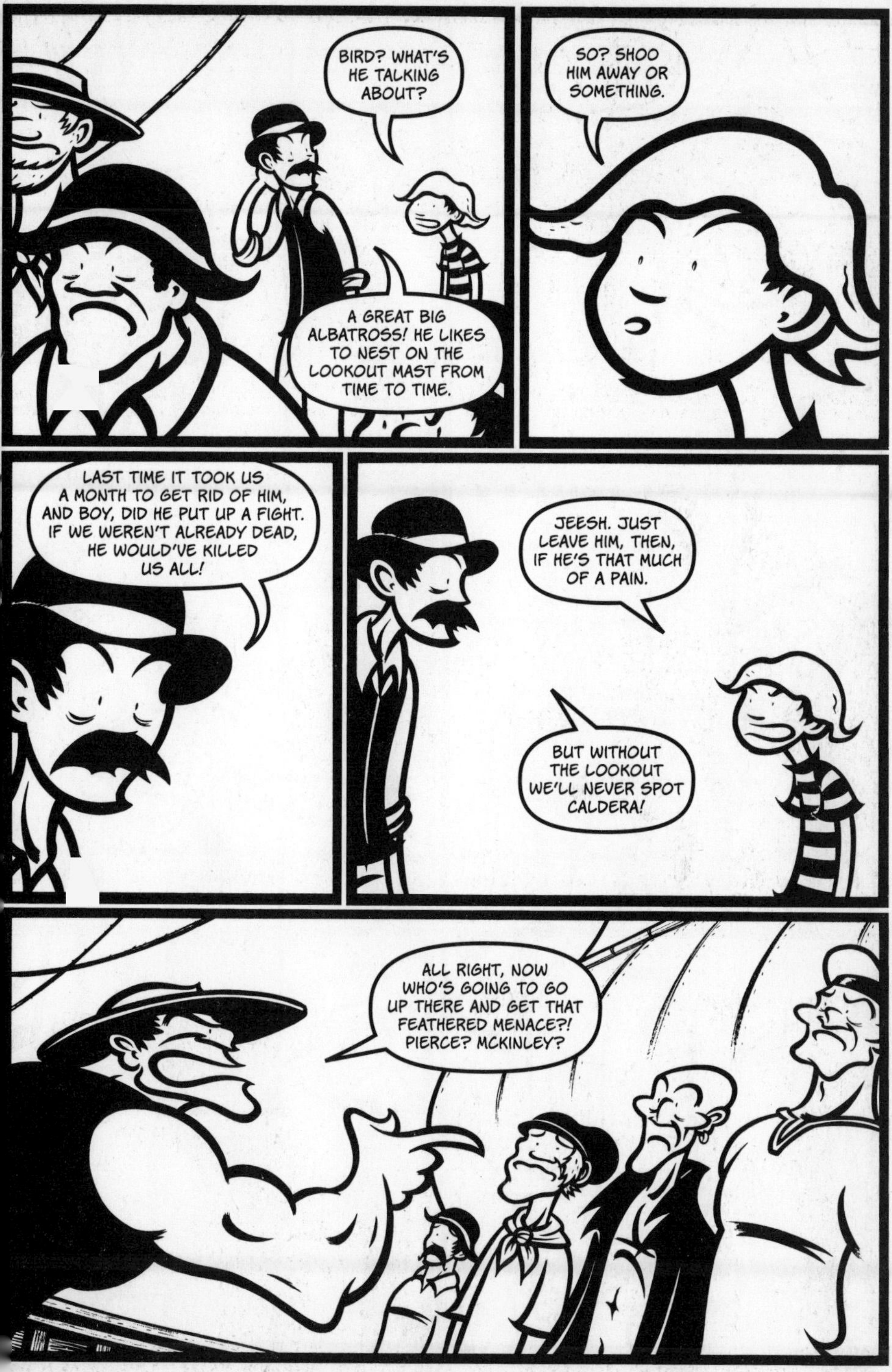
BIRD? WHAT'S HE TALKING ABOUT?
A GREAT BIG ALBATROSS! HE LIKES TO NEST ON THE LOOKOUT MAST FROM TIME TO TIME.
SO? SHOO HIM AWAY OR SOMETHING.
LAST TIME IT TOOK US A MONTH TO GET RID OF HIM, AND BOY, DID HE PUT UP A FIGHT. IF WE WEREN'T ALREADY DEAD, HE WOULD'VE KILLED US ALL!
JEESH. JUST LEAVE HIM, THEN, IF HE'S THAT MUCH OF A PAIN.
BUT WITHOUT THE LOOKOUT WE'LL NEVER SPOT CALDERA!
ALL RIGHT, NOW WHO'S GOING TO GO UP THERE AND GET THAT FEATHERED MENACE?! PIERCE? MCKINLEY?

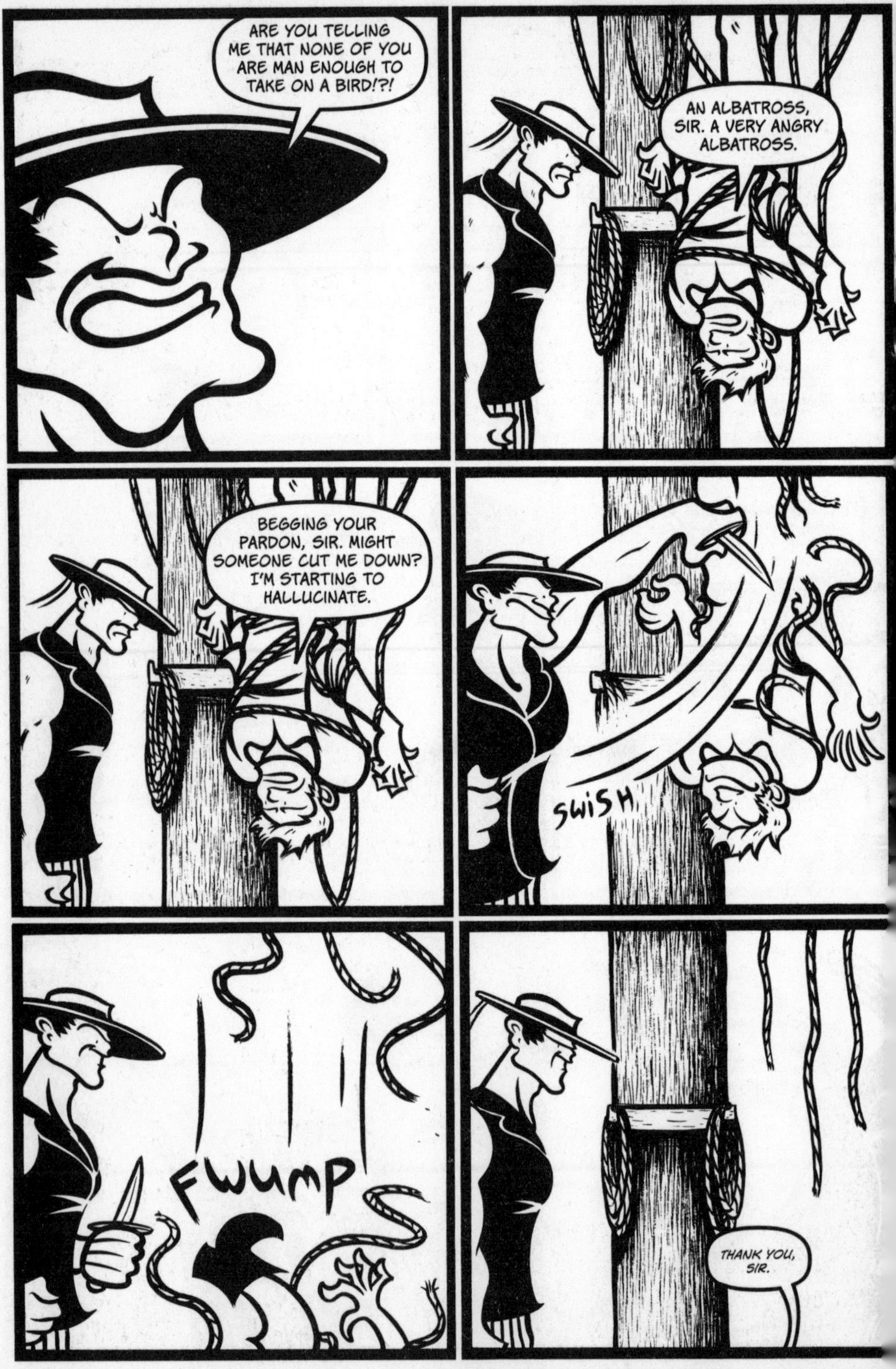
ARE YOU TELLING ME THAT NONE OF YOU ARE MAN ENOUGH TO TAKE ON A BIRD!?!
AN ALBATROSS, SIR. A VERY ANGRY ALBATROSS.
BEGGING YOUR PARDON, SIR. MIGHT SOMEONE CUT ME DOWN? I'M STARTING TO HALLUCINATE.
SWISH
FWUMP
THANK YOU, SIR.

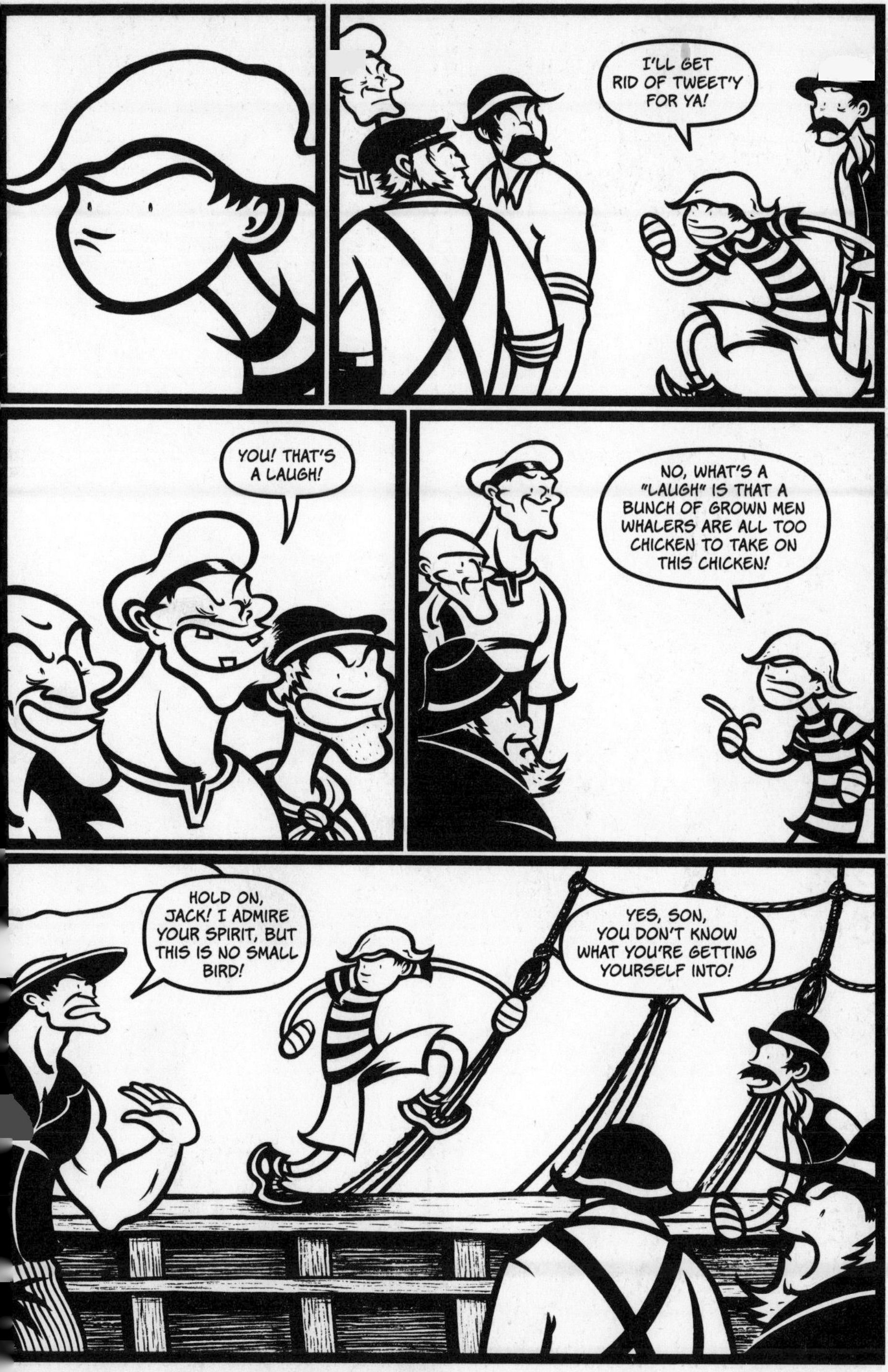
I'LL GET RID OF TWEET'Y FOR YA!
YOU! THAT'S A LAUGH!
NO, WHAT'S A "LAUGH" IS THAT A BUNCH OF GROWN MEN WHALERS ARE ALL TOO CHICKEN TO TAKE ON THIS CHICKEN!
HOLD ON, JACK! I ADMIRE YOUR SPIRIT, BUT THIS IS NO SMALL BIRD!
YES, SON, YOU DON'T KNOW WHAT YOU'RE GETTING YOURSELF INTO!

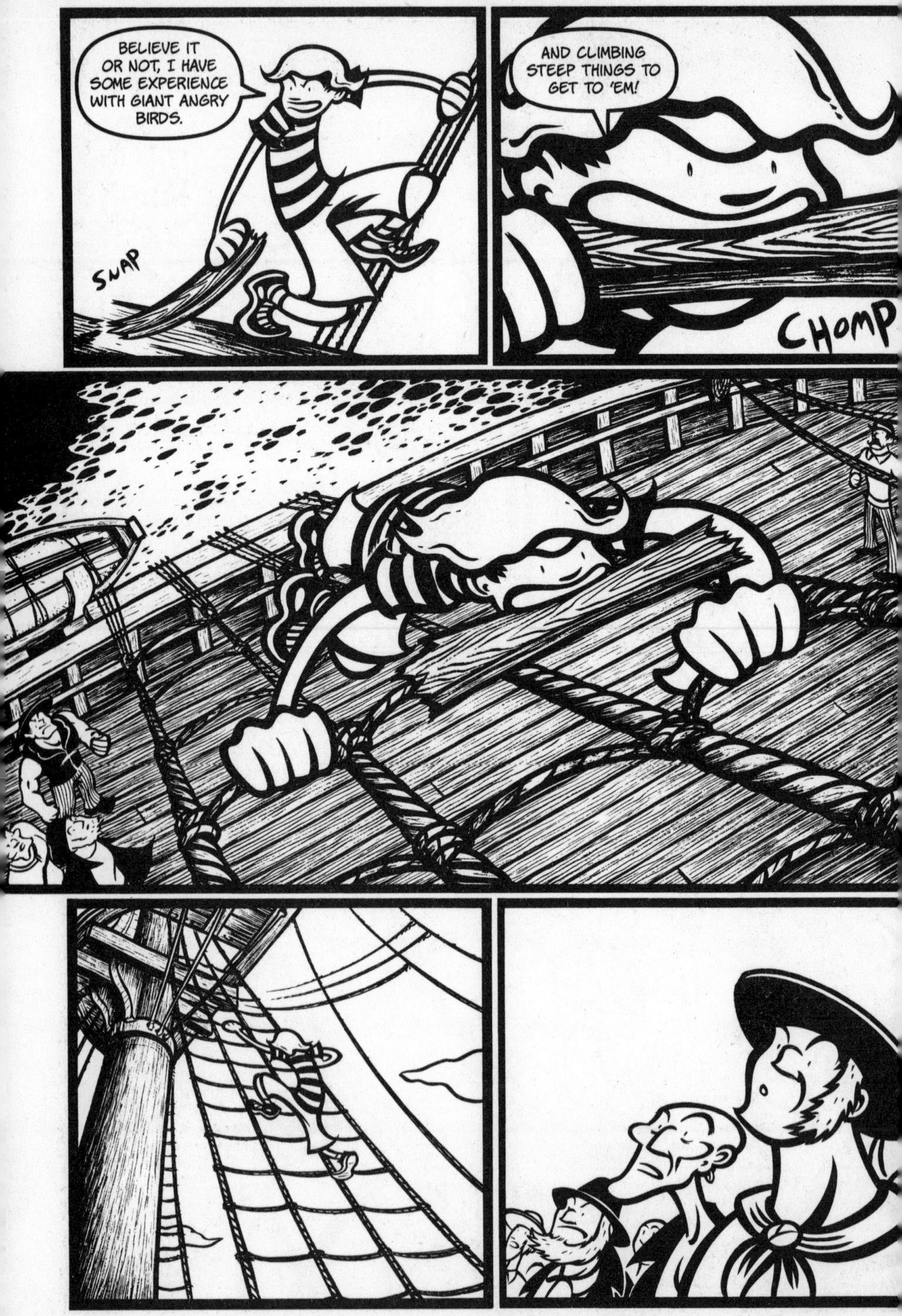
BELIEVE IT OR NOT, I HAVE SOME EXPERIENCE WITH GIANT ANGRY BIRDS.
SNAP
AND CLIMBING STEEP THINGS TO GET TO 'EM!
CHOMP

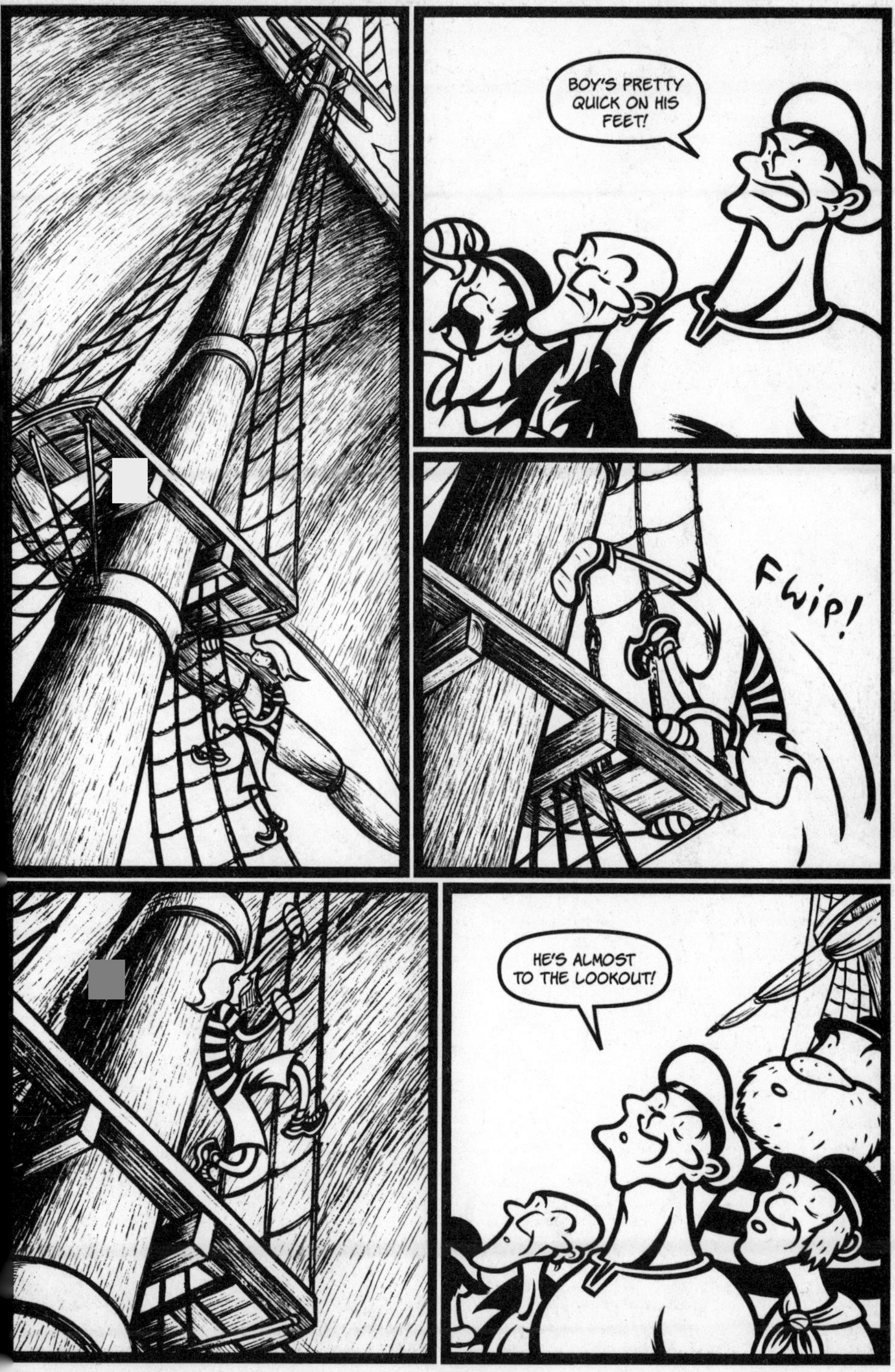
BOY'S PRETTY QUICK ON HIS FEET!
FWIP!
HE'S ALMOST TO THE LOOKOUT!

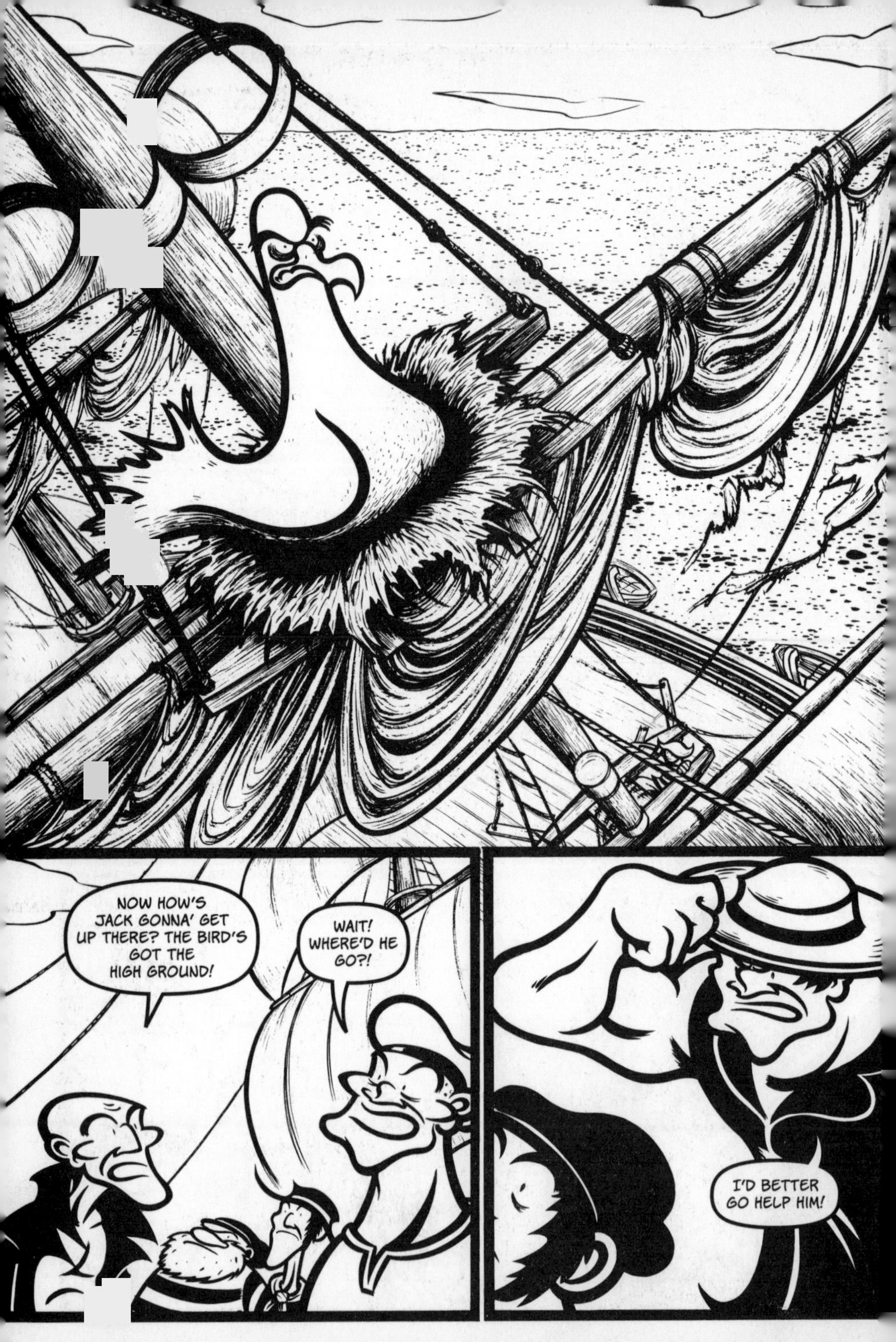
NOW HOW'S JACK GONNA' GET UP THERE? THE BIRD'S GOT THE HIGH GROUND!
WAIT! WHERE'D HE GO?!
I'D BETTER GO HELP HIM!

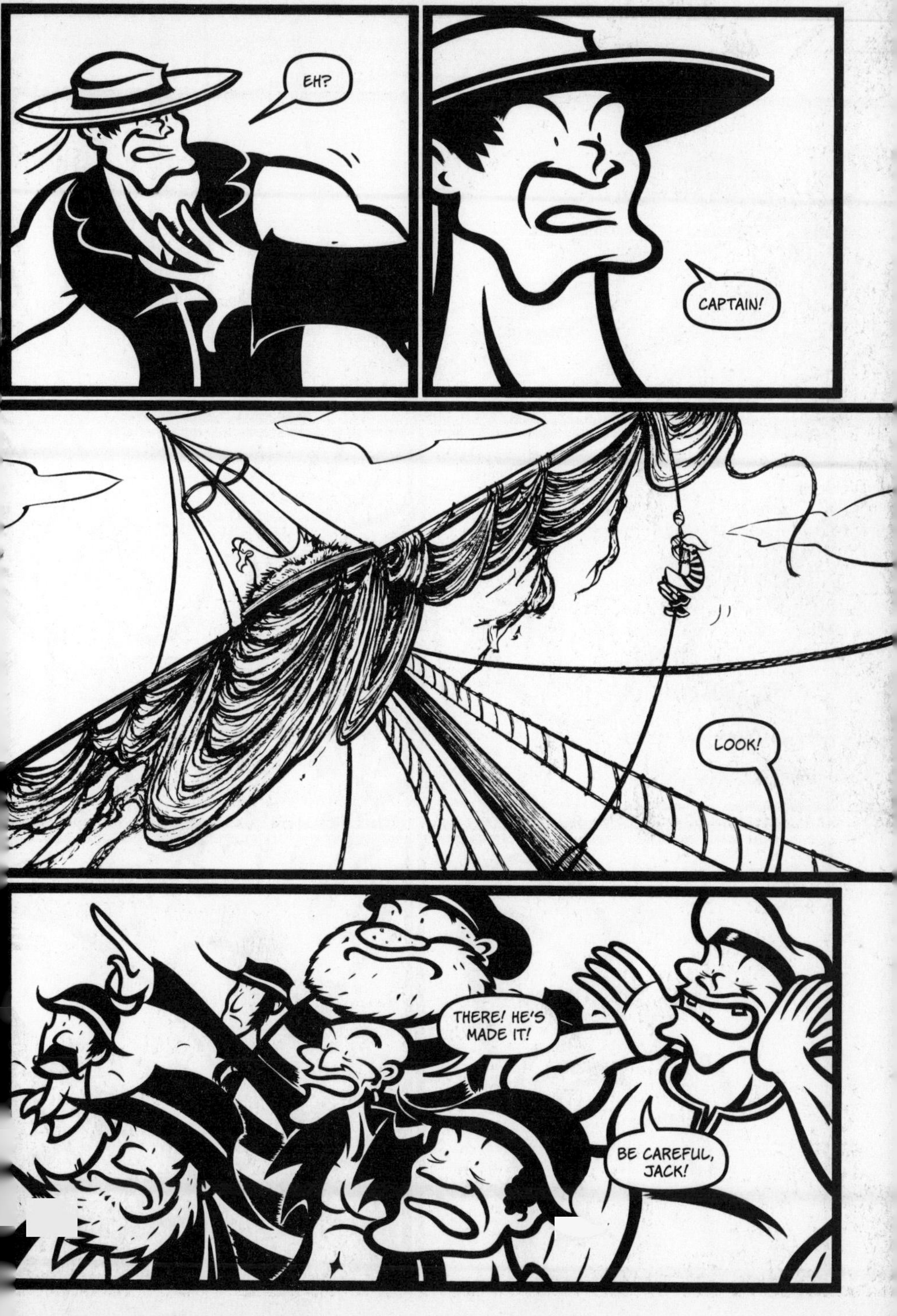
EH?
CAPTAIN!
LOOK!
THERE! HE'S MADE IT!
BE CAREFUL, JACK!

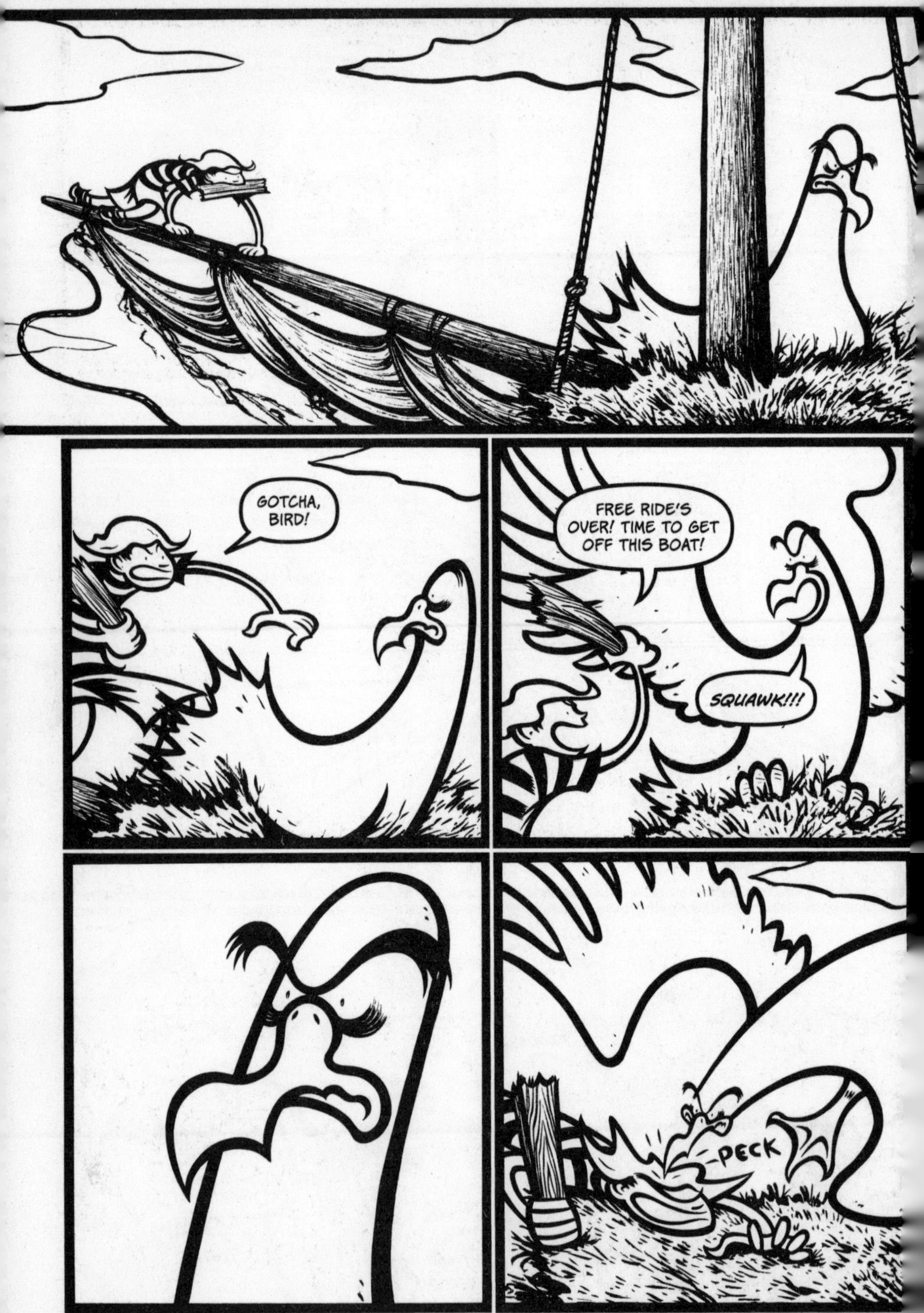
GOTCHA, BIRD!
FREE RIDE'S OVER! TIME TO GET OFF THIS BOAT!
SQUAWK!!!
PECK

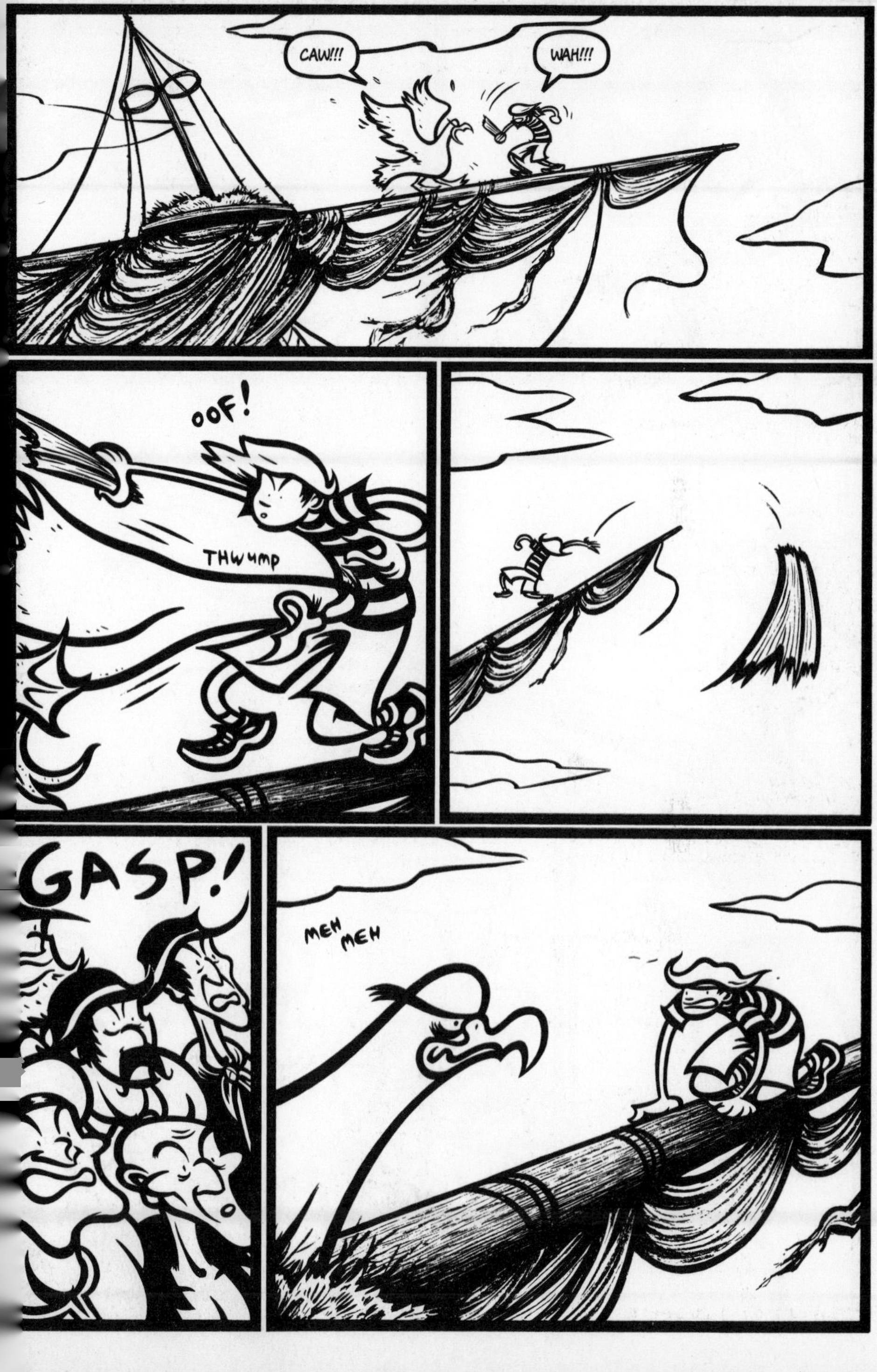
CAW!!!
WAH!!!
OOF!
THWUMP
GASP!
MEH
MEH

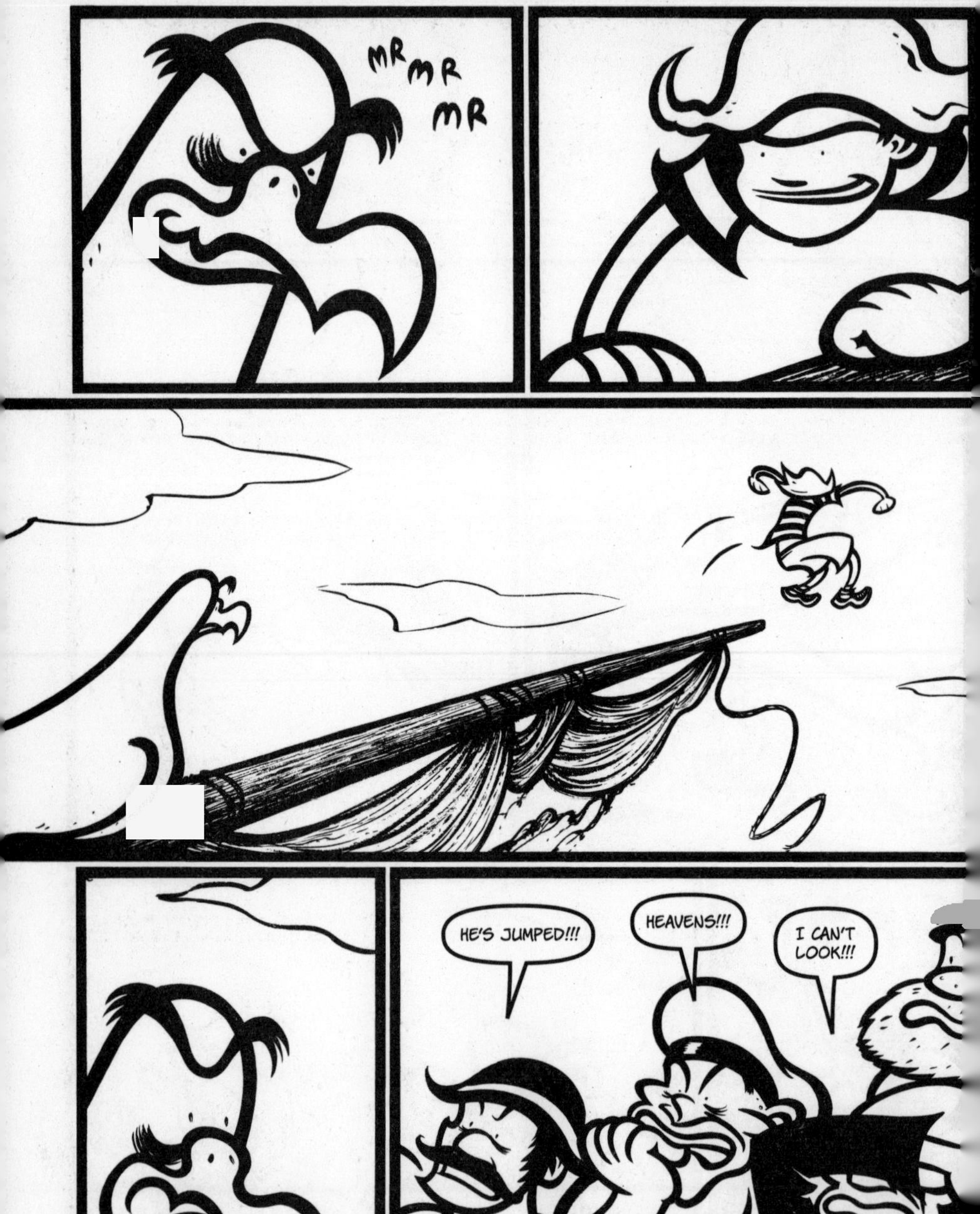
MR MR MR
HE'S JUMPED!!!
HEAVENS!!!
I CAN'T LOOK!!!

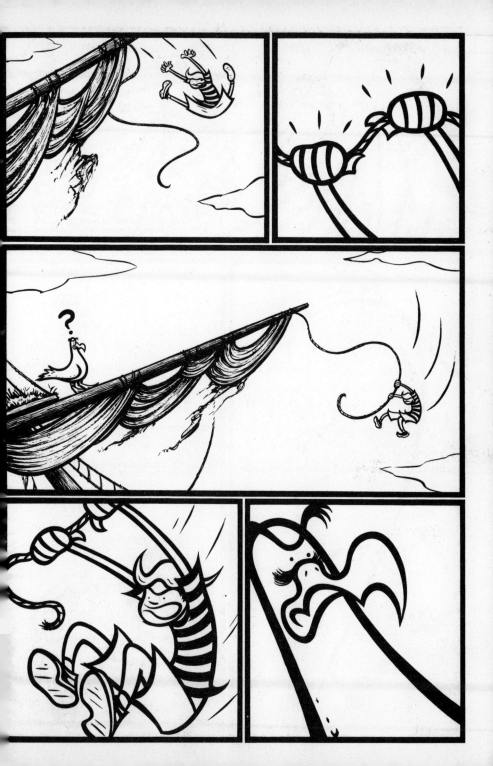

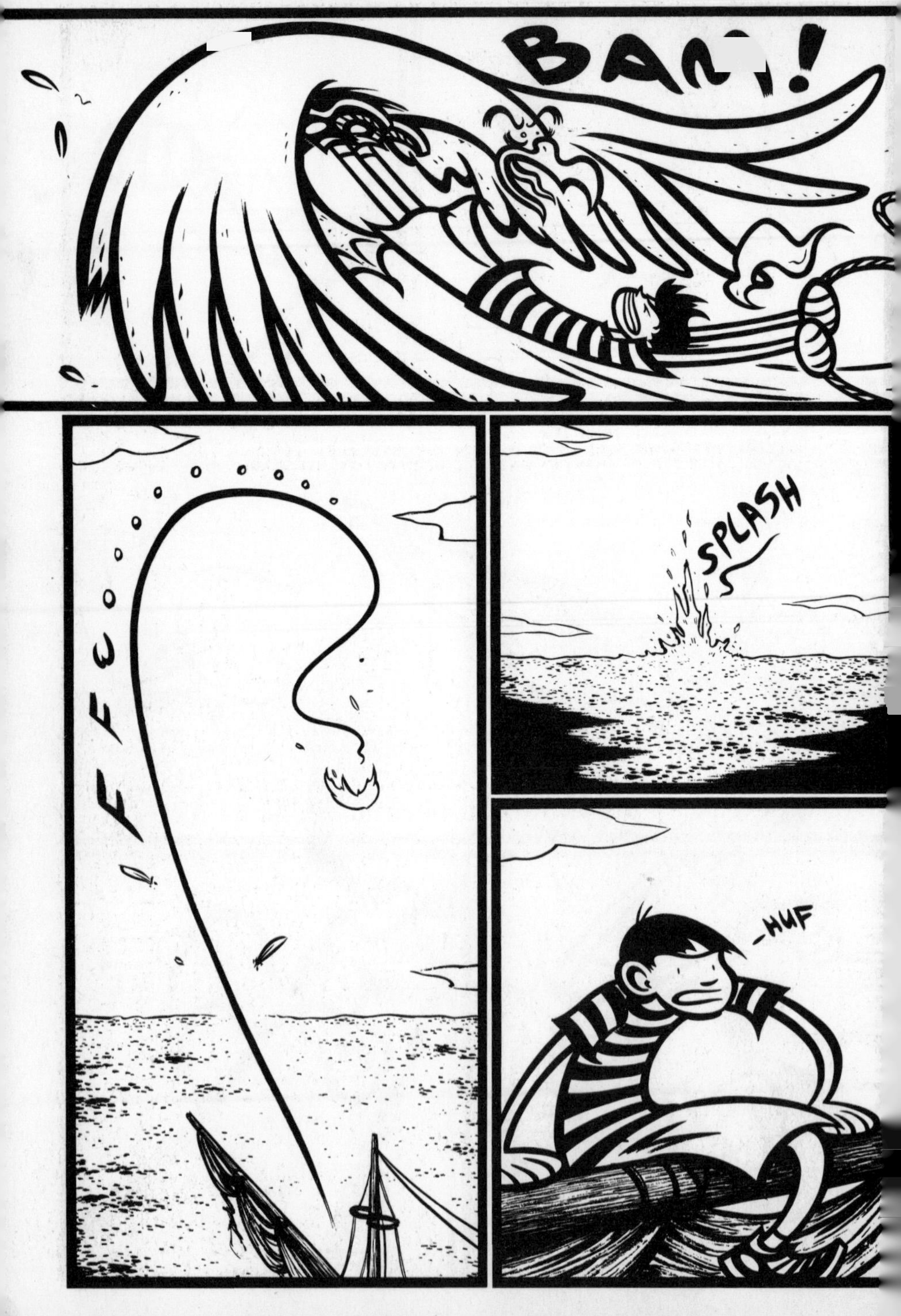
BAM!
FFWOOOOOOOOOO
SPLASH
-HUF

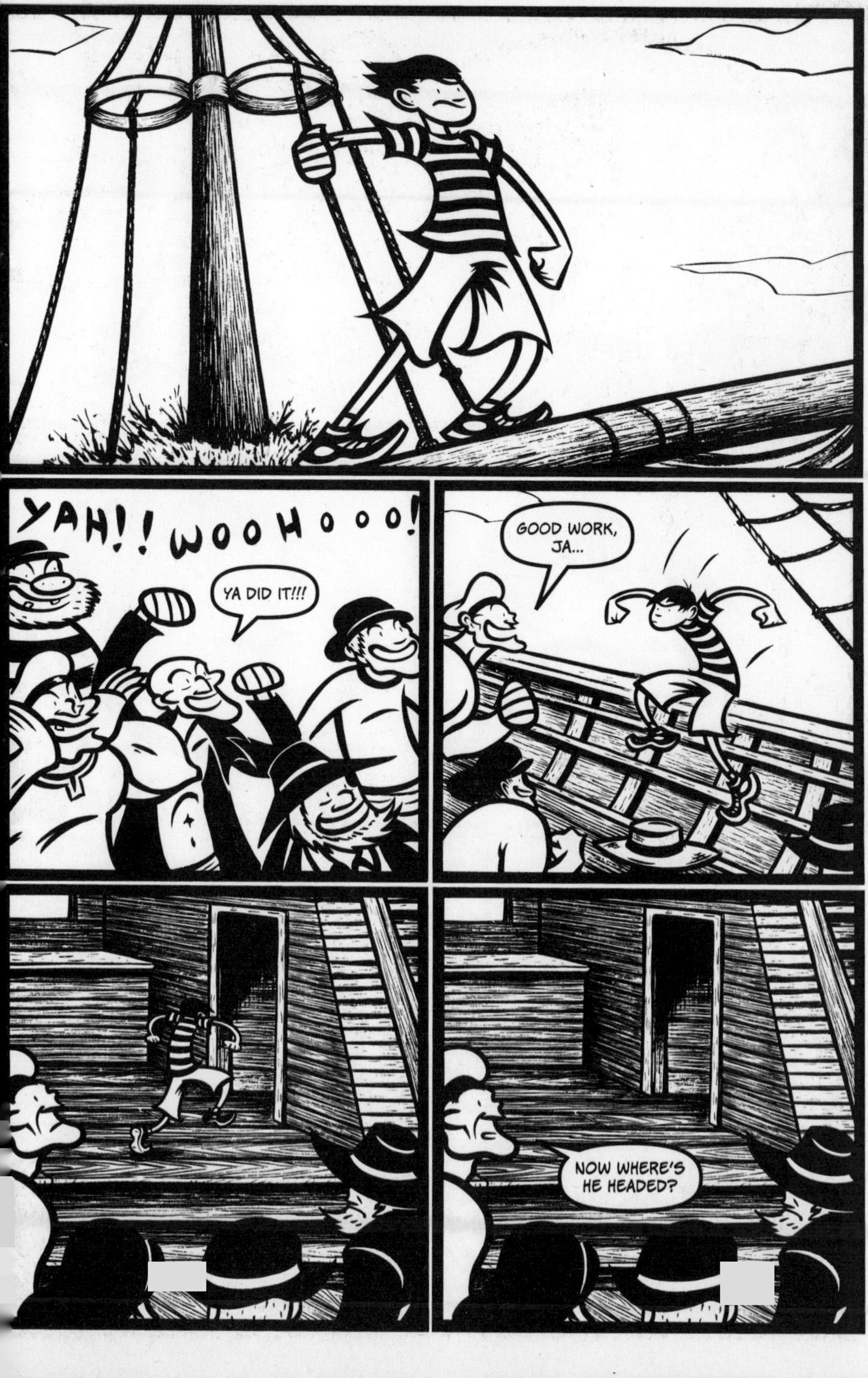
YAH!! WOOHOOO!
YA DID IT!!!
GOOD WORK, JA...
NOW WHERE'S HE HEADED?

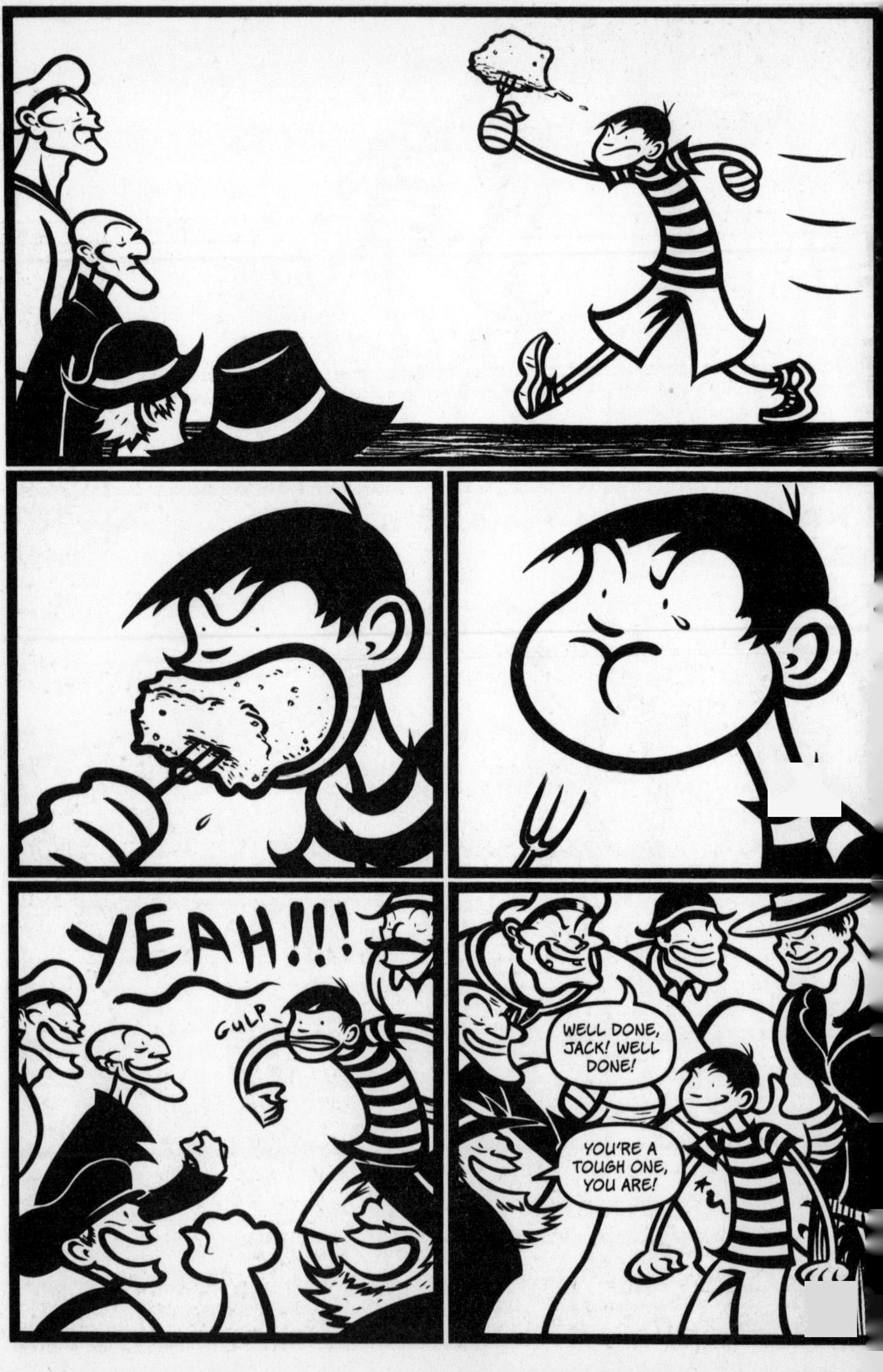
YEAH!!!
GULP
WELL DONE, JACK! WELL DONE!
YOU'RE A TOUGH ONE, YOU ARE!

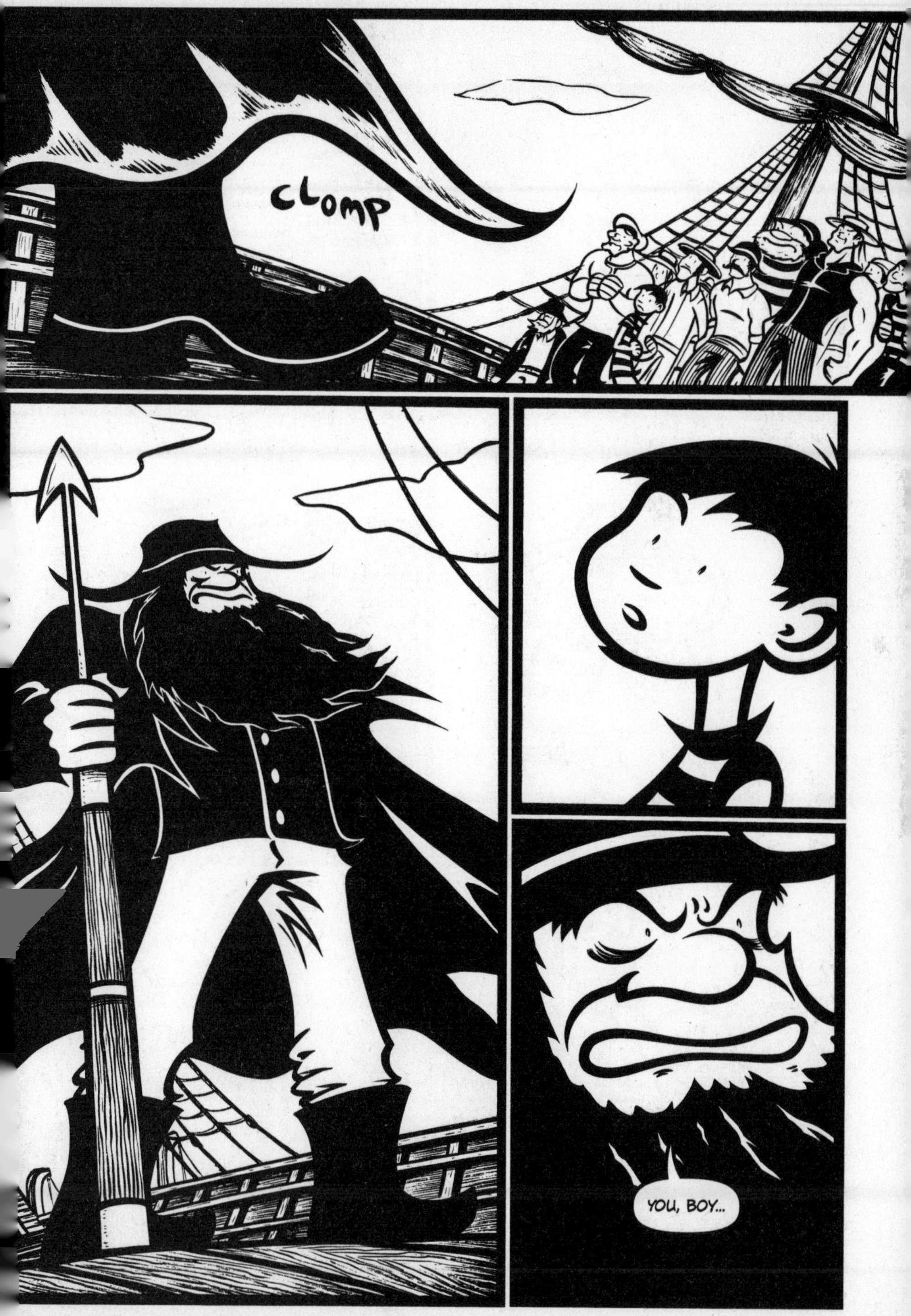
CLOMP
YOU, BOY...

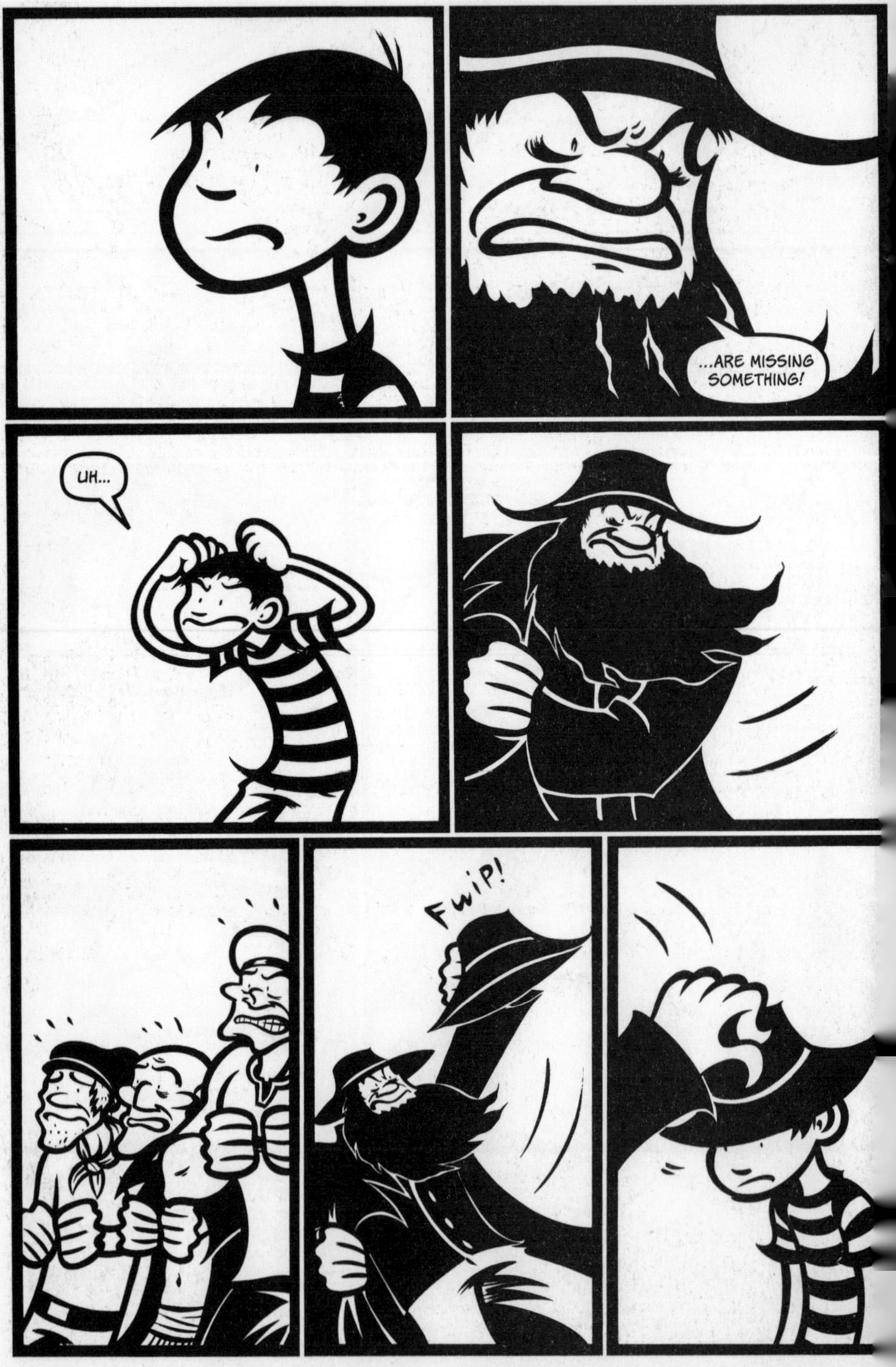
...ARE MISSING SOMETHING!
UH...
FWIP!

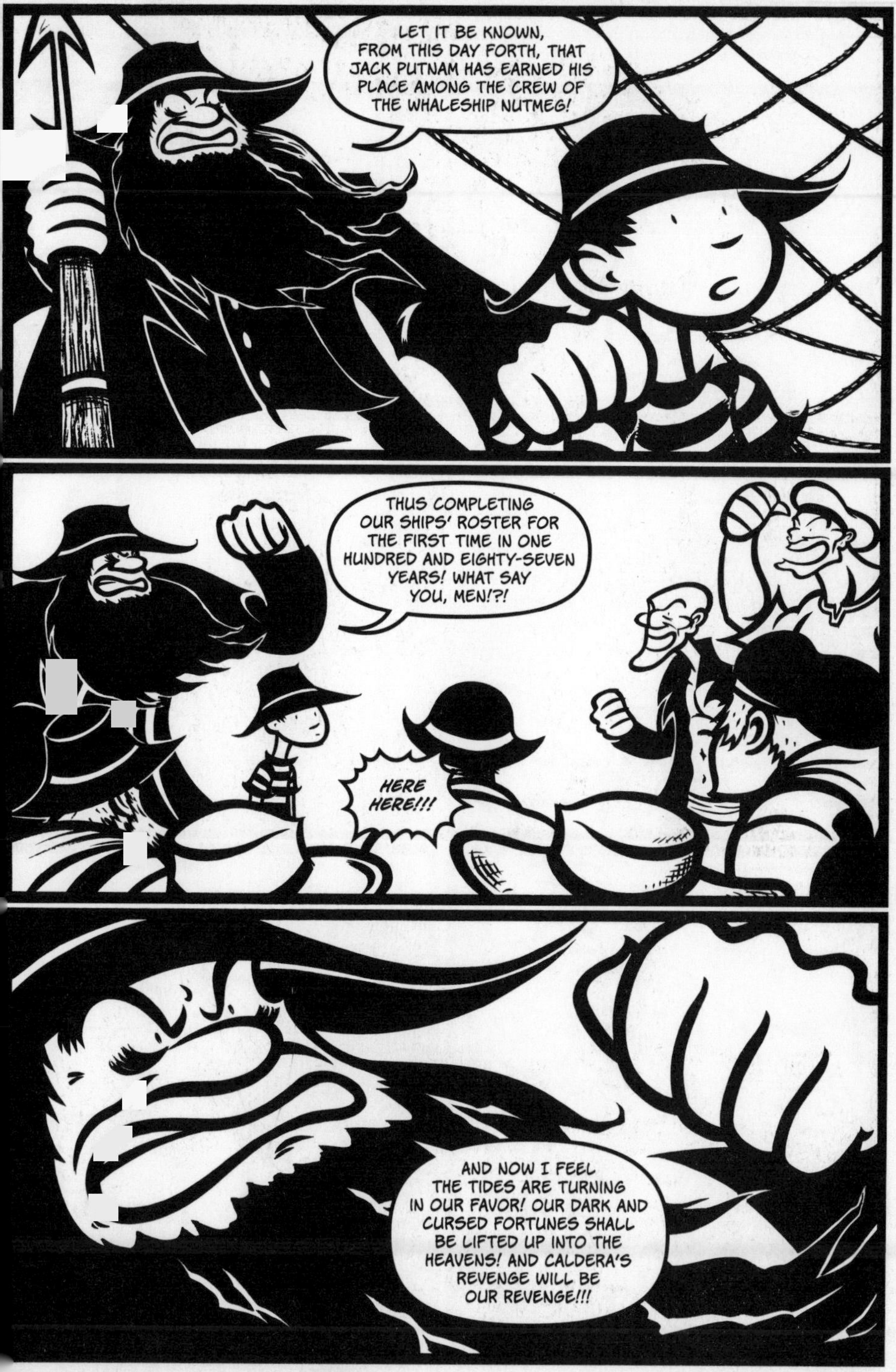
LET IT BE KNOWN, FROM THIS DAY FORTH, THAT JACK PUTNAM HAS EARNED HIS PLACE AMONG THE CREW OF THE WHALESHIP NUTMEG!
THUS COMPLETING OUR SHIPS' ROSTER FOR THE FIRST TIME IN ONE HUNDRED AND EIGHTY-SEVEN YEARS! WHAT SAY YOU, MEN!?!
HERE HERE!!!
AND NOW I FEEL THE TIDES ARE TURNING IN OUR FAVOR! OUR DARK AND CURSED FORTUNES SHALL BE LIFTED UP INTO THE HEAVENS! AND CALDERA'S REVENGE WILL BE OUR REVENGE!!!

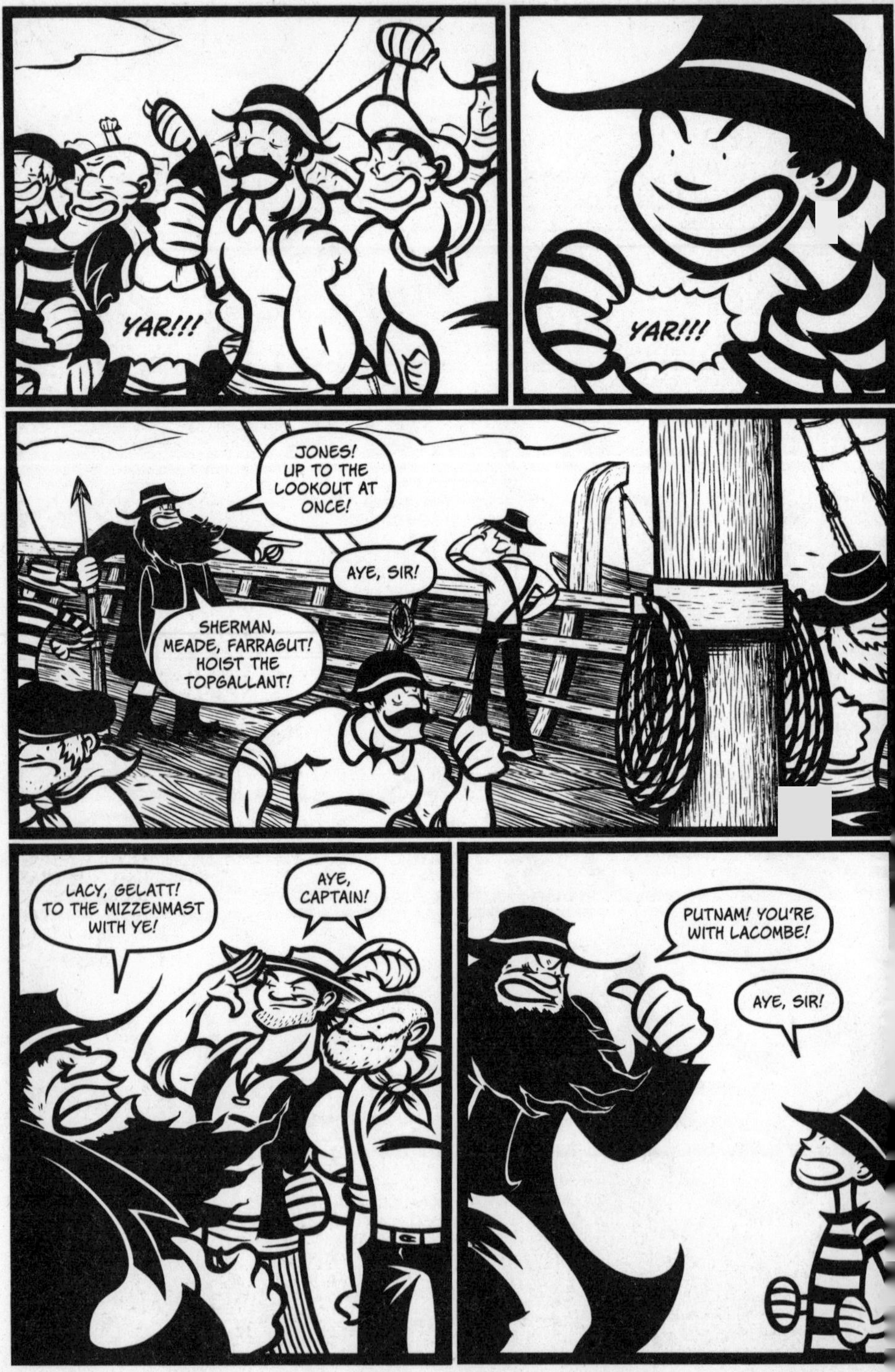
YAR!!!
YAR!!!
JONES! UP TO THE LOOKOUT AT ONCE!
AYE, SIR!
SHERMAN, MEADE, FARRAGUT! HOIST THE TOPGALLANT!
LACY, GELATT! TO THE MIZZENMAST WITH YE!
AYE, CAPTAIN!
PUTNAM! YOU'RE WITH LACOMBE!
AYE, SIR!

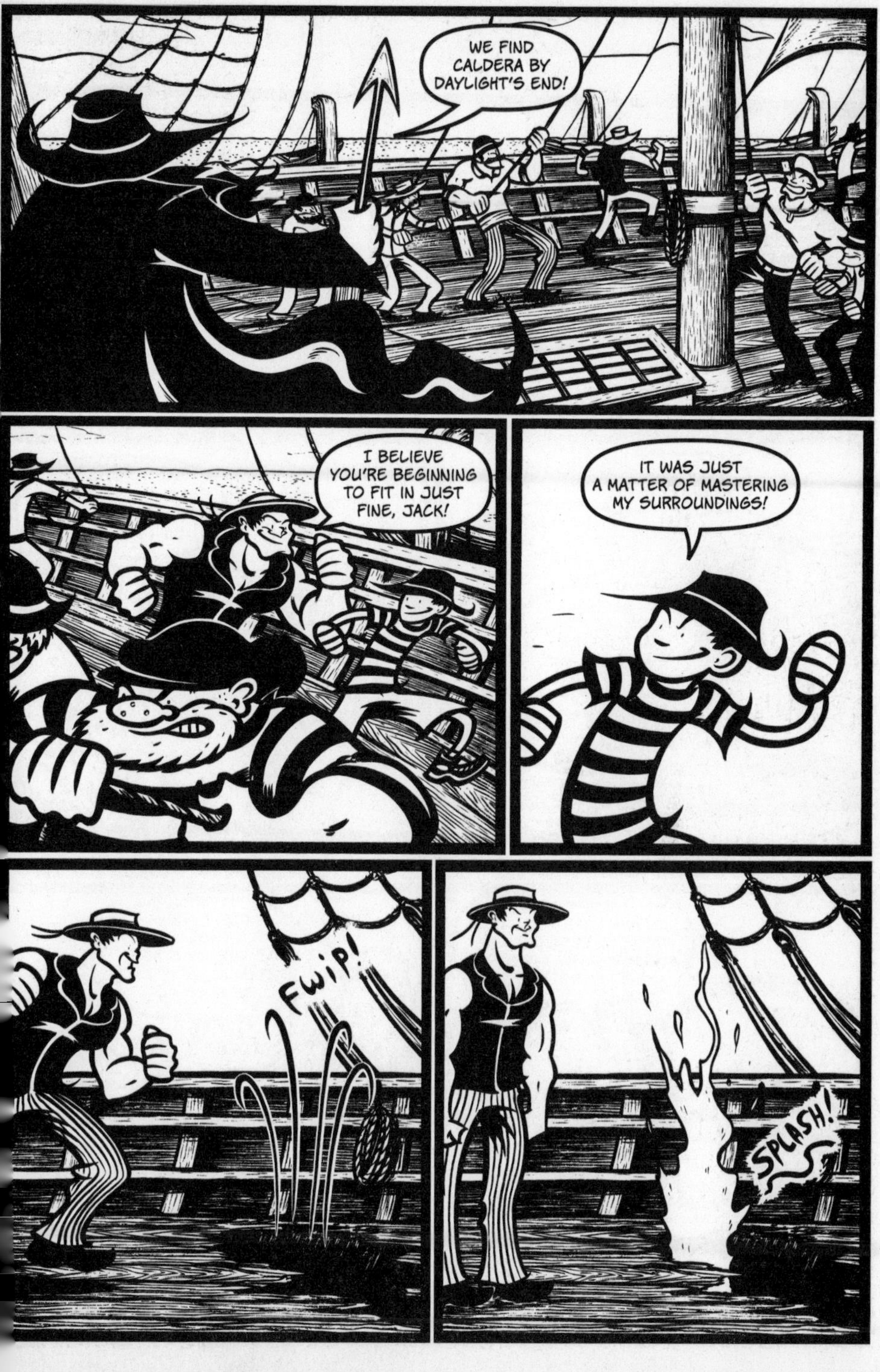

WE FIND CALDERA BY DAYLIGHT'S END!
I BELIEVE YOU'RE BEGINNING TO FIT IN JUST FINE, JACK!
IT WAS JUST A MATTER OF MASTERING MY SURROUNDINGS!
FWIP!
SPLASH!

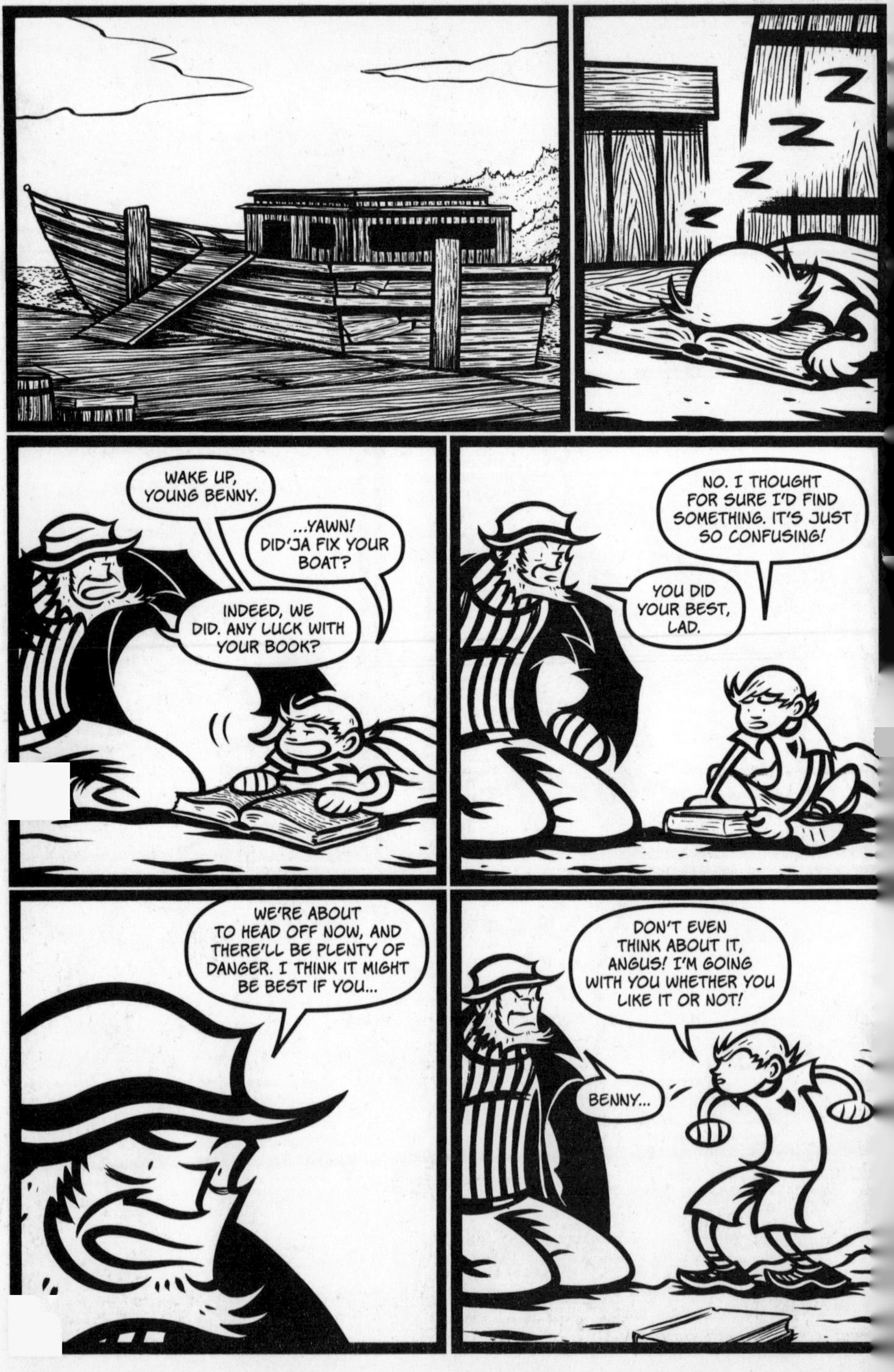
Z
Z
Z
Z
WAKE UP, YOUNG BENNY.
...YAWN! DID'JA FIX YOUR BOAT?
INDEED, WE DID. ANY LUCK WITH YOUR BOOK?
NO. I THOUGHT FOR SURE I'D FIND SOMETHING. IT'S JUST SO CONFUSING!
YOU DID YOUR BEST, LAD.
WE'RE ABOUT TO HEAD OFF NOW, AND THERE'LL BE PLENTY OF DANGER. I THINK IT MIGHT BE BEST IF YOU...
DON'T EVEN THINK ABOUT IT, ANGUS! I'M GOING WITH YOU WHETHER YOU LIKE IT OR NOT!
BENNY...

I'M NOT GONNA ABANDON MY BROTHER TO CRAZY GHOST WHALERS AND THEIR GIANT CRAZY WHALE, I DON'T CARE HOW DANGEROUS THEY ARE!

PLUS, YOU CAN'T HAVE *ALL* THE ADVENTURING TO YOURSELF. THAT WOULD JUST BE GREEDY OF YOU.

WELL, THAT SETTLES THAT, THEN.

YES IT DOES.

BENNY!

SUNNY!!!

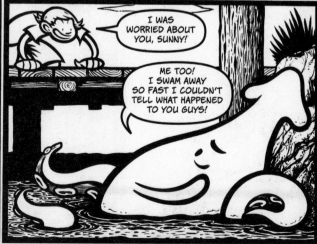

I WAS WORRIED ABOUT YOU, SUNNY!

ME TOO! I SWAM AWAY SO FAST I COULDN'T TELL WHAT HAPPENED TO YOU GUYS!

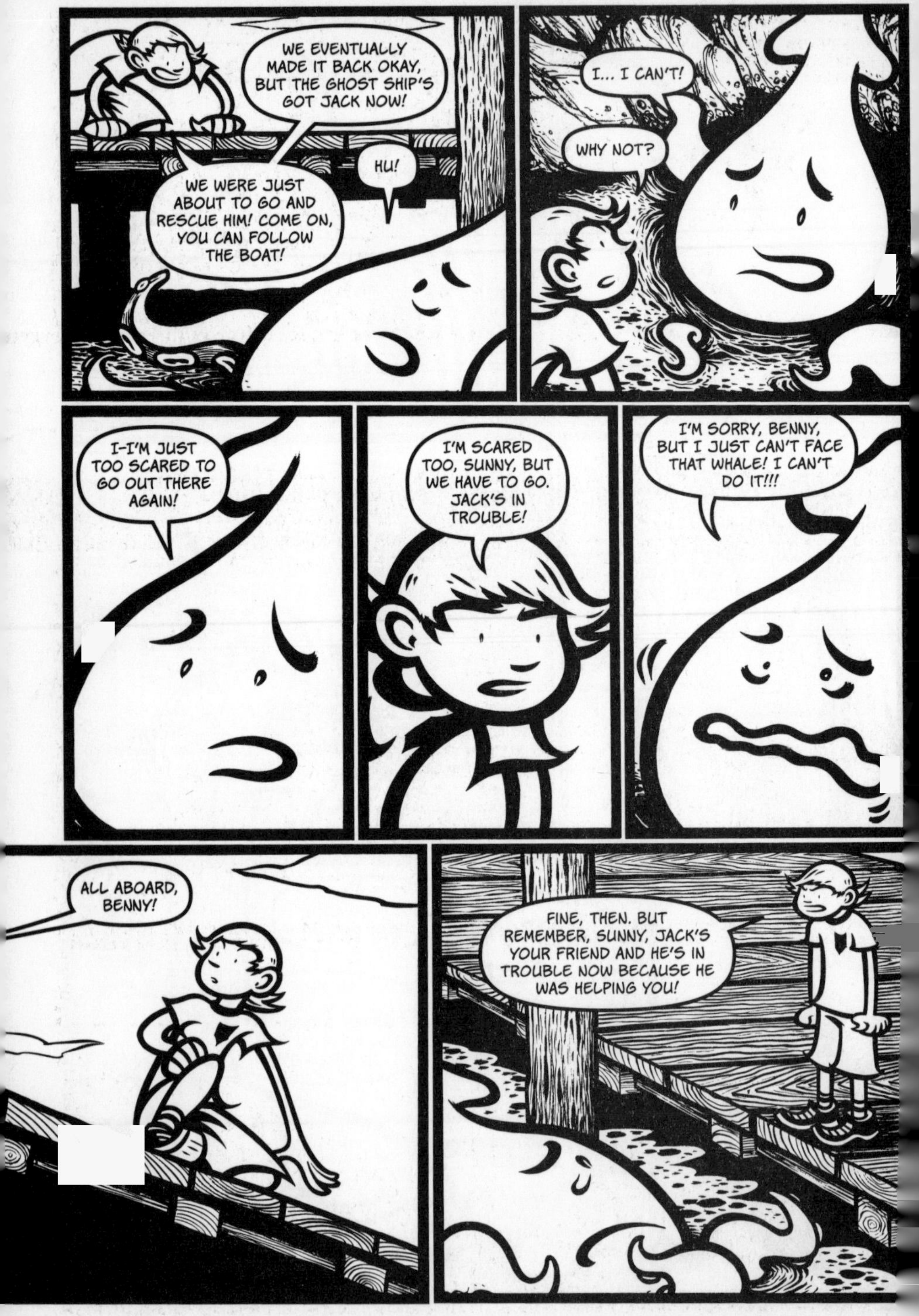
WE EVENTUALLY MADE IT BACK OKAY, BUT THE GHOST SHIP'S GOT JACK NOW!
WE WERE JUST ABOUT TO GO AND RESCUE HIM! COME ON, YOU CAN FOLLOW THE BOAT!
HU!
I... I CAN'T!
WHY NOT?
I-I'M JUST TOO SCARED TO GO OUT THERE AGAIN!
I'M SCARED TOO, SUNNY, BUT WE HAVE TO GO. JACK'S IN TROUBLE!
I'M SORRY, BENNY, BUT I JUST CAN'T FACE THAT WHALE! I CAN'T DO IT!!!
ALL ABOARD, BENNY!
FINE, THEN. BUT REMEMBER, SUNNY, JACK'S YOUR FRIEND AND HE'S IN TROUBLE NOW BECAUSE HE WAS HELPING YOU!

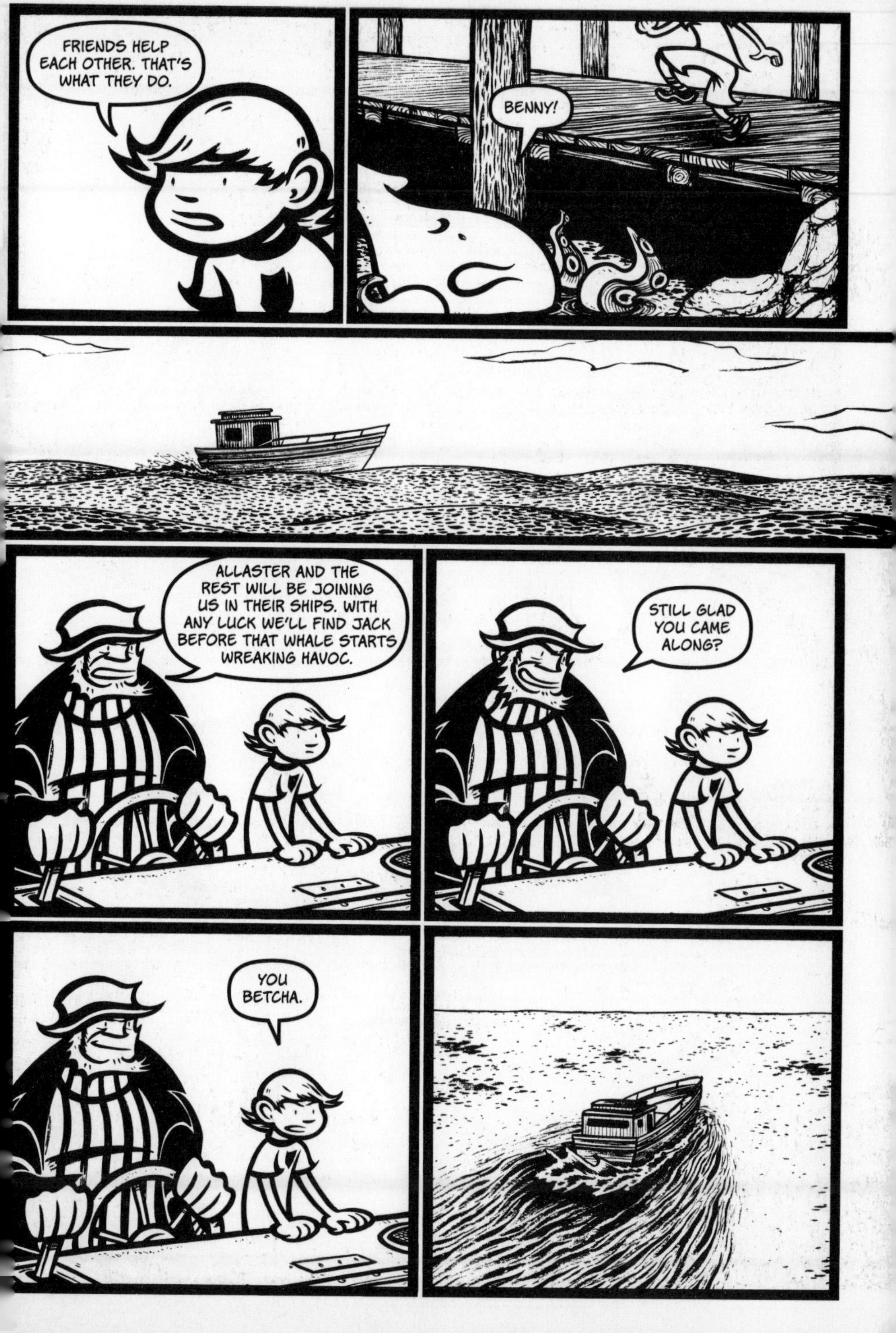
FRIENDS HELP EACH OTHER. THAT'S WHAT THEY DO.
BENNY!
ALLASTER AND THE REST WILL BE JOINING US IN THEIR SHIPS. WITH ANY LUCK WE'LL FIND JACK BEFORE THAT WHALE STARTS WREAKING HAVOC.
STILL GLAD YOU CAME ALONG?
YOU BETCHA.

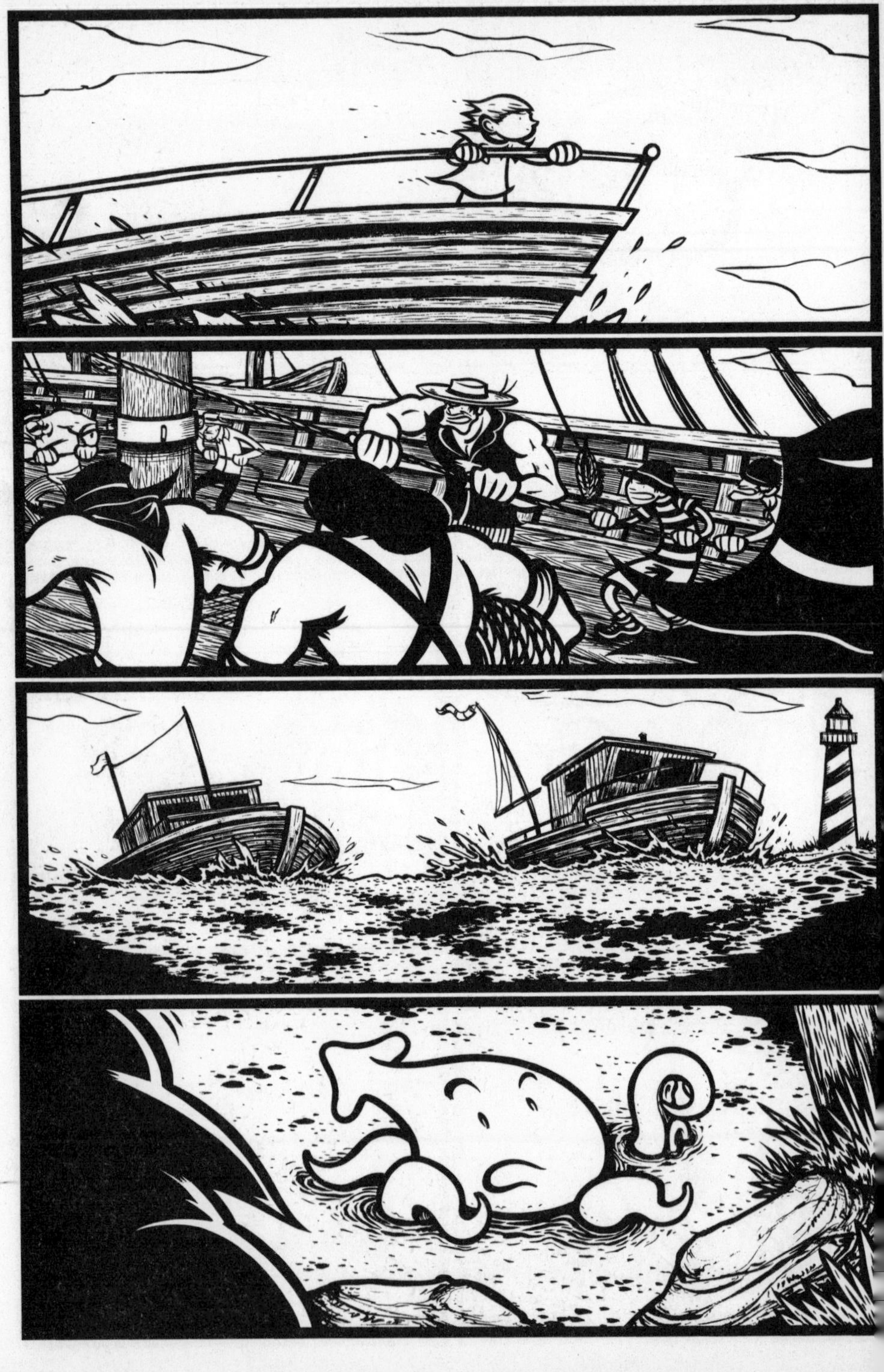

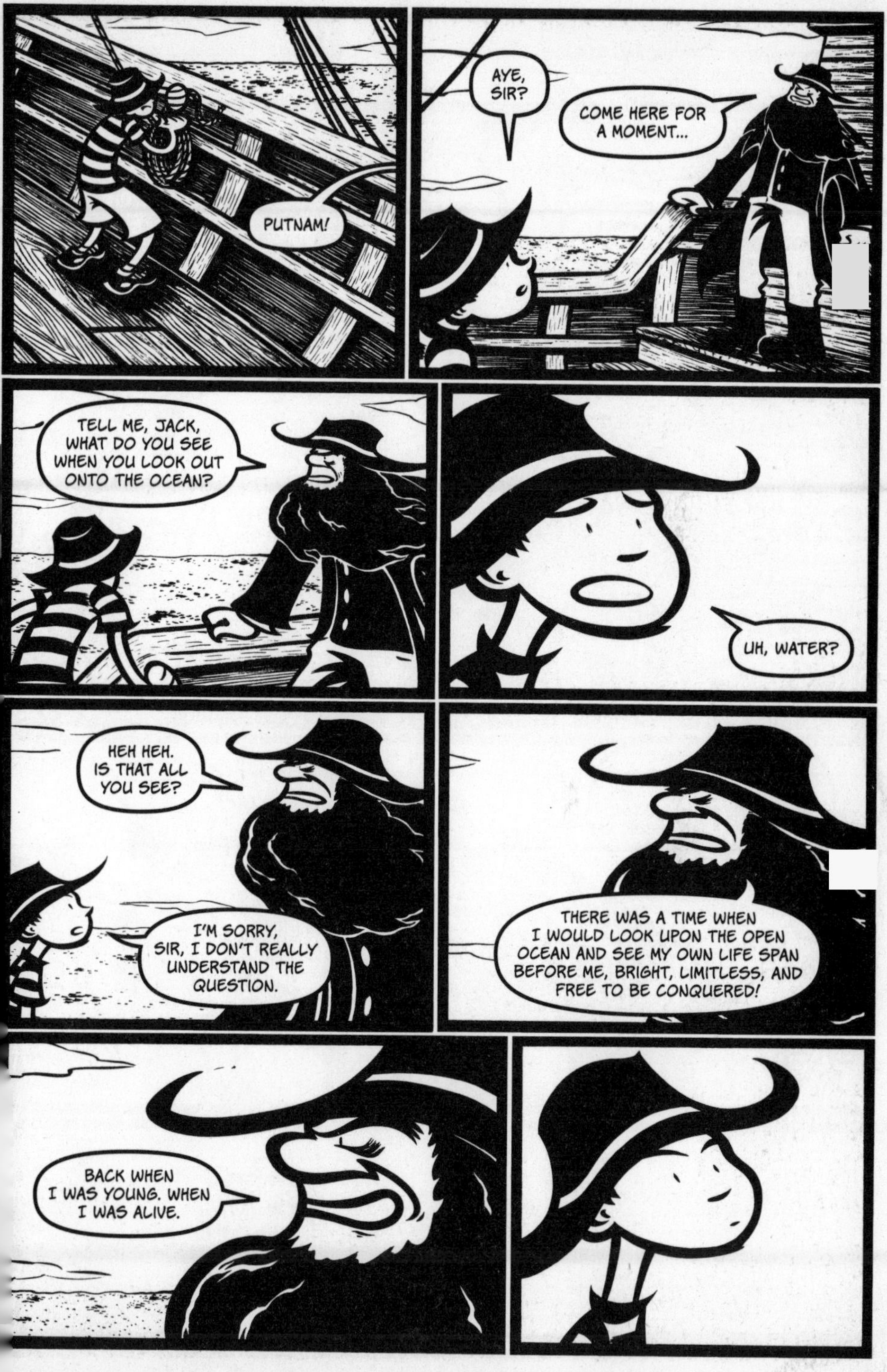
PUTNAM!
AYE, SIR?
COME HERE FOR A MOMENT...
TELL ME, JACK, WHAT DO YOU SEE WHEN YOU LOOK OUT ONTO THE OCEAN?
UH, WATER?
HEH HEH. IS THAT ALL YOU SEE?
I'M SORRY, SIR, I DON'T REALLY UNDERSTAND THE QUESTION.
THERE WAS A TIME WHEN I WOULD LOOK UPON THE OPEN OCEAN AND SEE MY OWN LIFE SPAN BEFORE ME, BRIGHT, LIMITLESS, AND FREE TO BE CONQUERED!
BACK WHEN I WAS YOUNG. WHEN I WAS ALIVE.

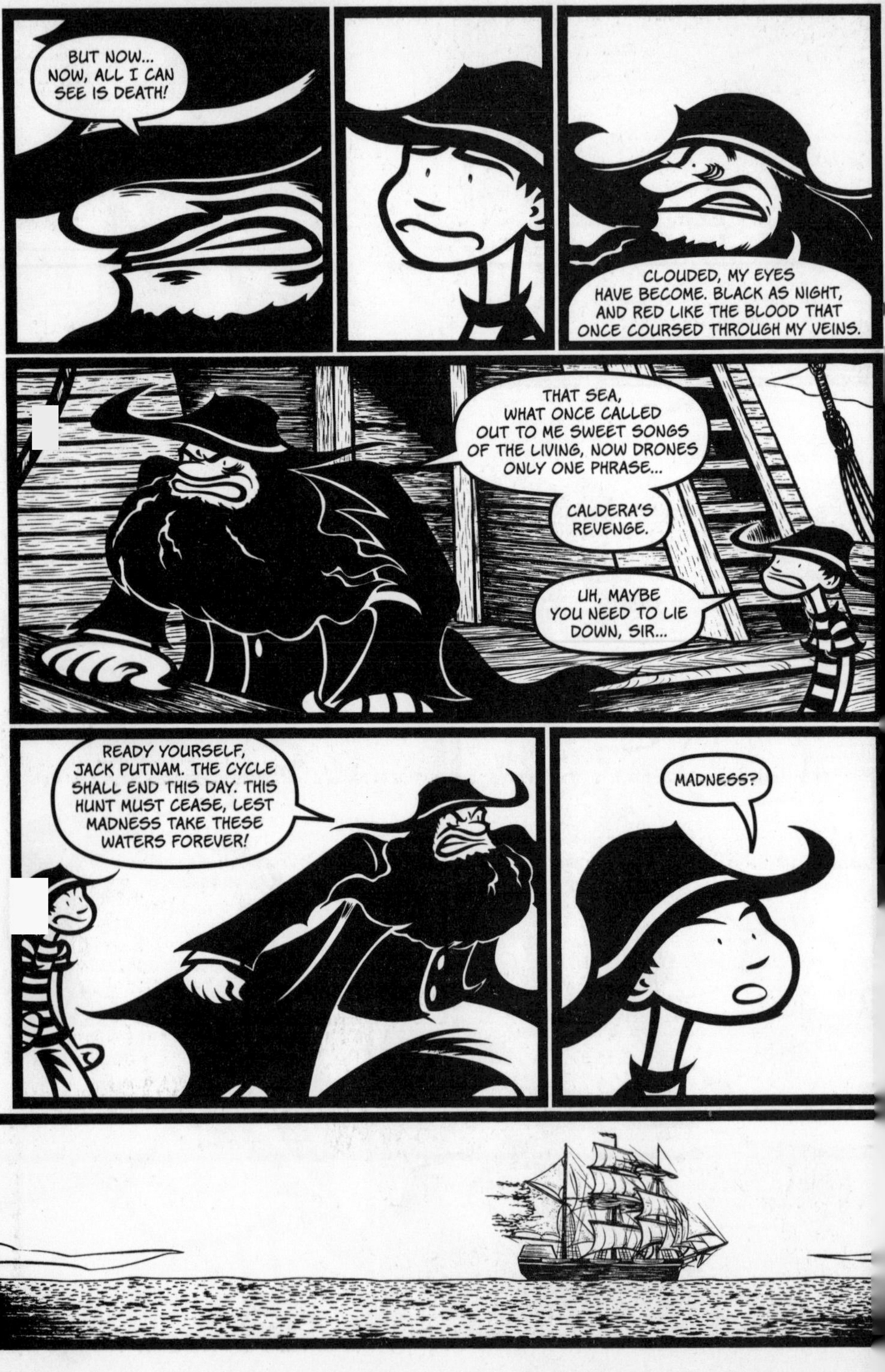
BUT NOW... NOW, ALL I CAN SEE IS DEATH!
CLOUDED, MY EYES HAVE BECOME. BLACK AS NIGHT, AND RED LIKE THE BLOOD THAT ONCE COURSED THROUGH MY VEINS.
THAT SEA, WHAT ONCE CALLED OUT TO ME SWEET SONGS OF THE LIVING, NOW DRONES ONLY ONE PHRASE...
CALDERA'S REVENGE.
UH, MAYBE YOU NEED TO LIE DOWN, SIR...
READY YOURSELF, JACK PUTNAM. THE CYCLE SHALL END THIS DAY. THIS HUNT MUST CEASE, LEST MADNESS TAKE THESE WATERS FOREVER!
MADNESS?

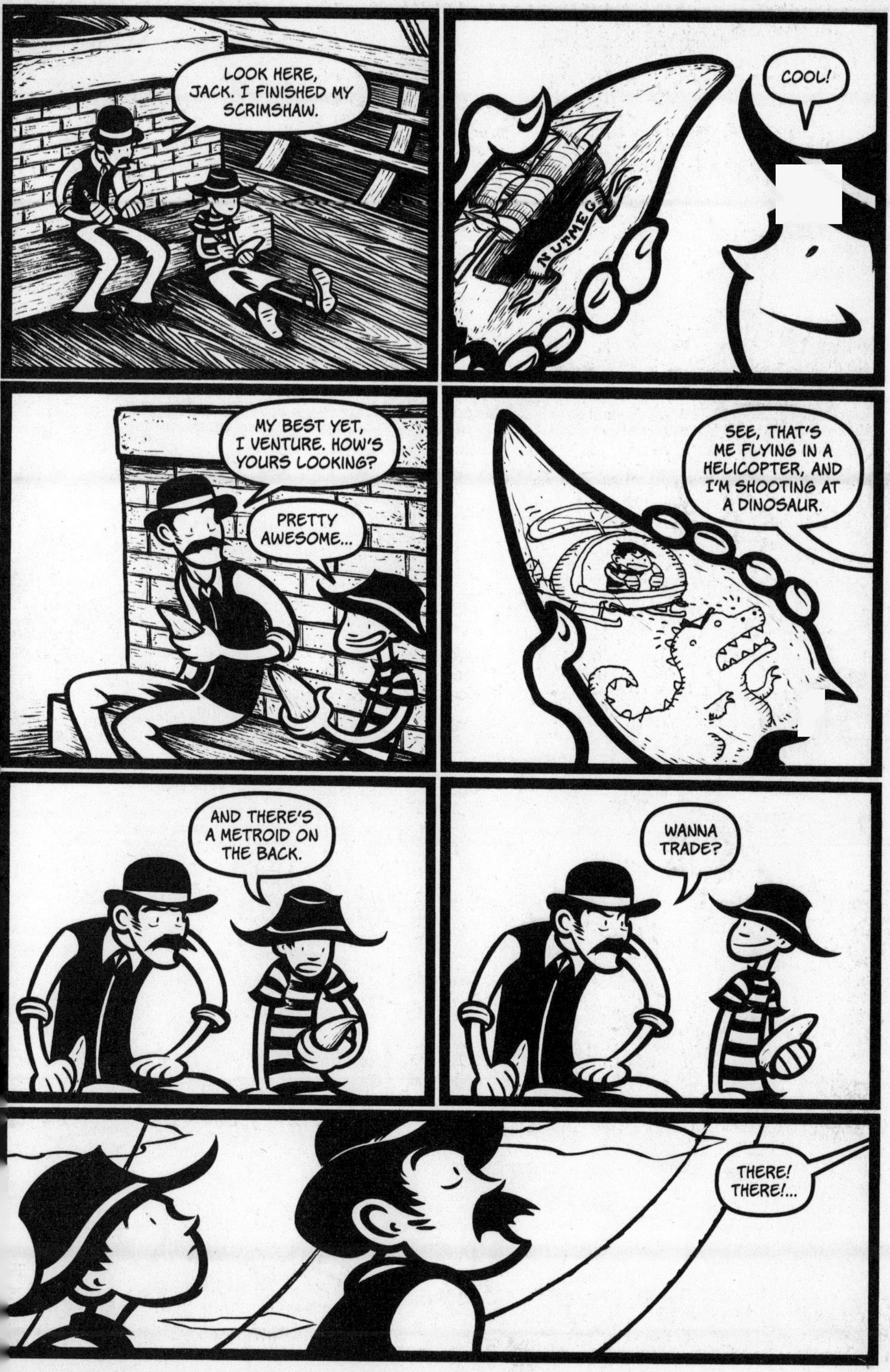
LOOK HERE, JACK. I FINISHED MY SCRIMSHAW.
COOL!
NUTMEG
MY BEST YET, I VENTURE. HOW'S YOURS LOOKING?
PRETTY AWESOME...
SEE, THAT'S ME FLYING IN A HELICOPTER, AND I'M SHOOTING AT A DINOSAUR.
AND THERE'S A METROID ON THE BACK.
WANNA TRADE?
THERE! THERE!...

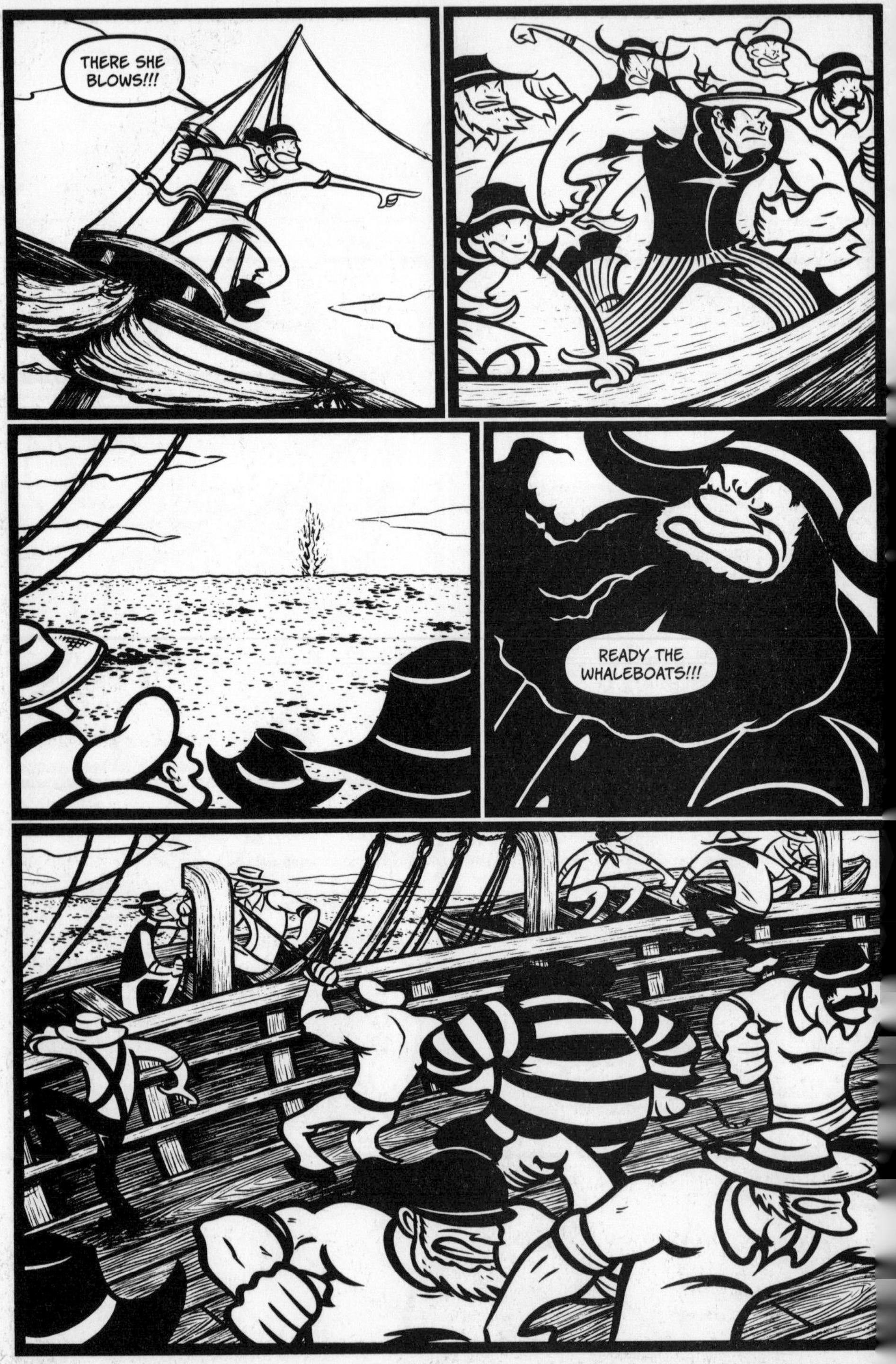
THERE SHE BLOWS!!!
READY THE WHALEBOATS!!!

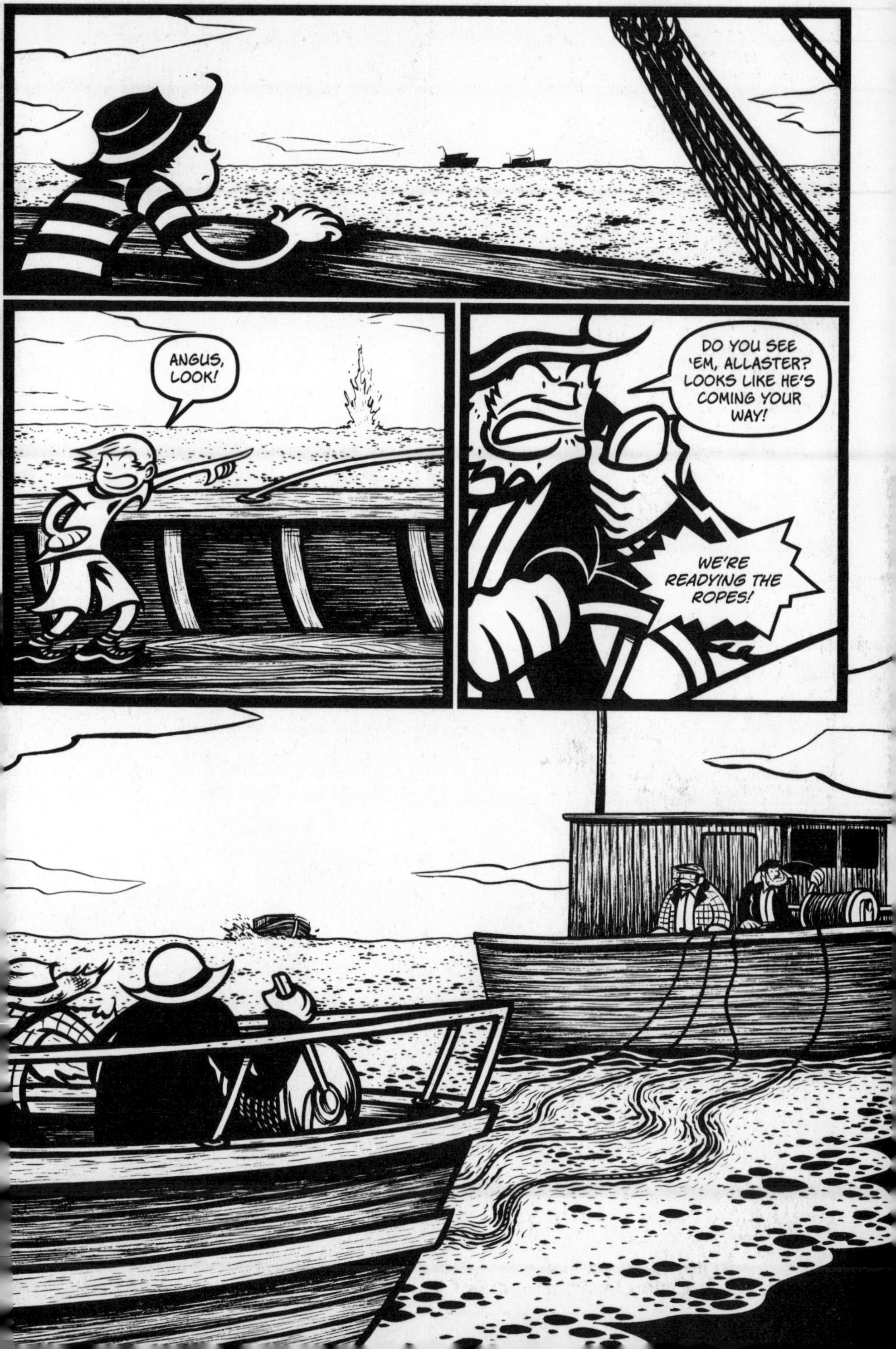
ANGUS, LOOK!
DO YOU SEE 'EM, ALLASTER? LOOKS LIKE HE'S COMING YOUR WAY!
WE'RE READYING THE ROPES!

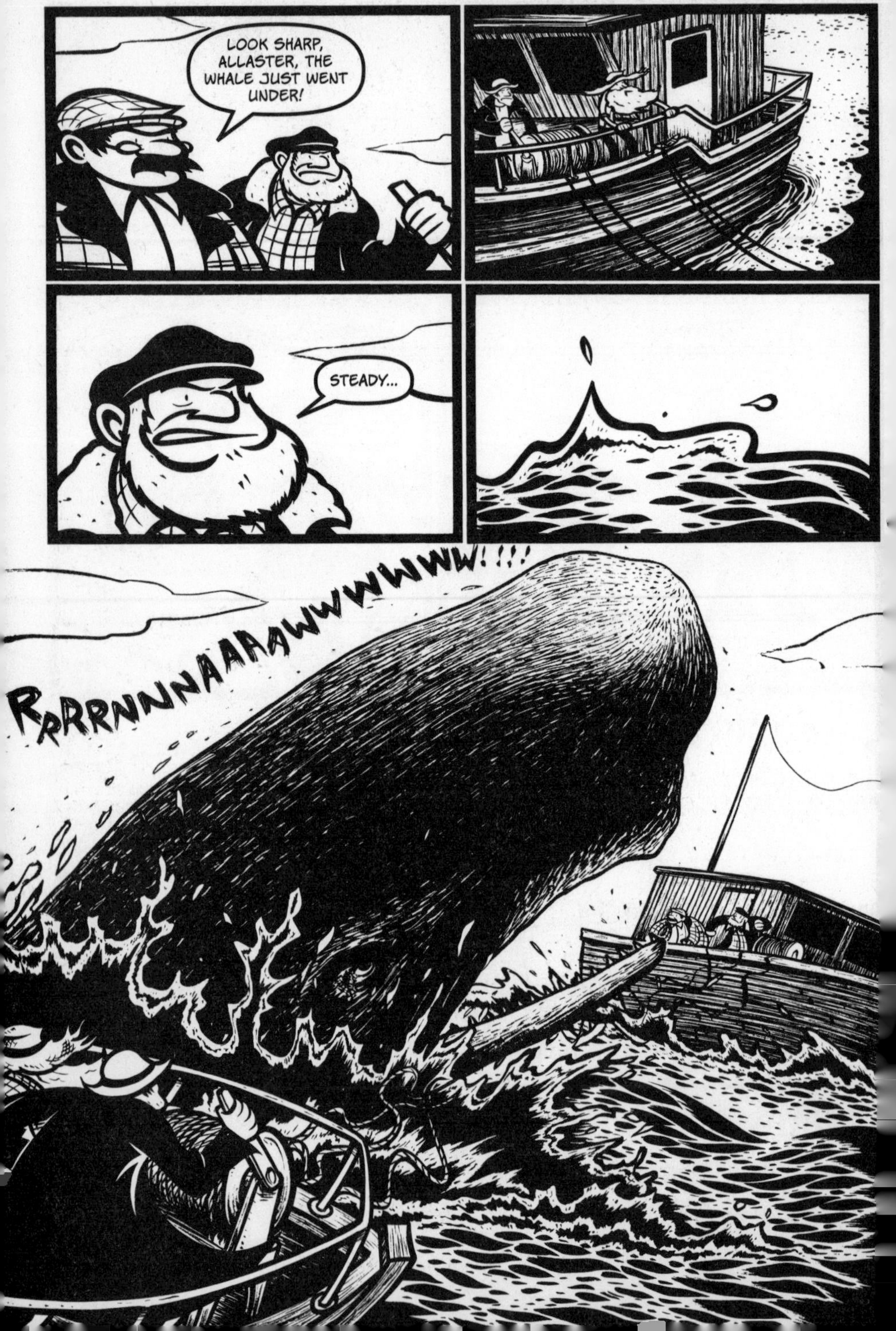
LOOK SHARP, ALLASTER, THE WHALE JUST WENT UNDER!
STEADY...
RRRRNNNAAAAWWWWWWW!!!!

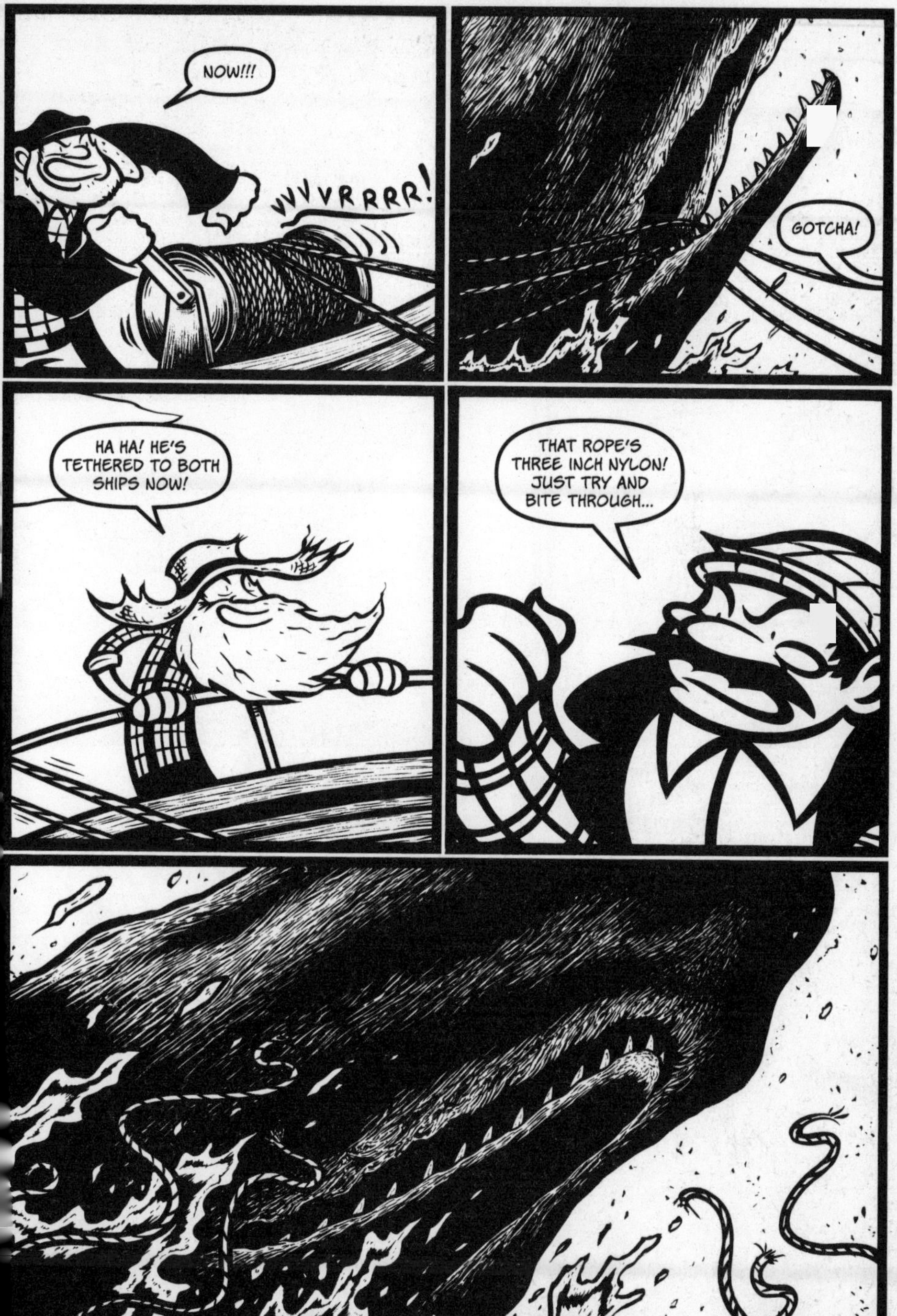
NOW!!!
VVVVRRRR!
GOTCHA!
HA HA! HE'S TETHERED TO BOTH SHIPS NOW!
THAT ROPE'S THREE INCH NYLON! JUST TRY AND BITE THROUGH...

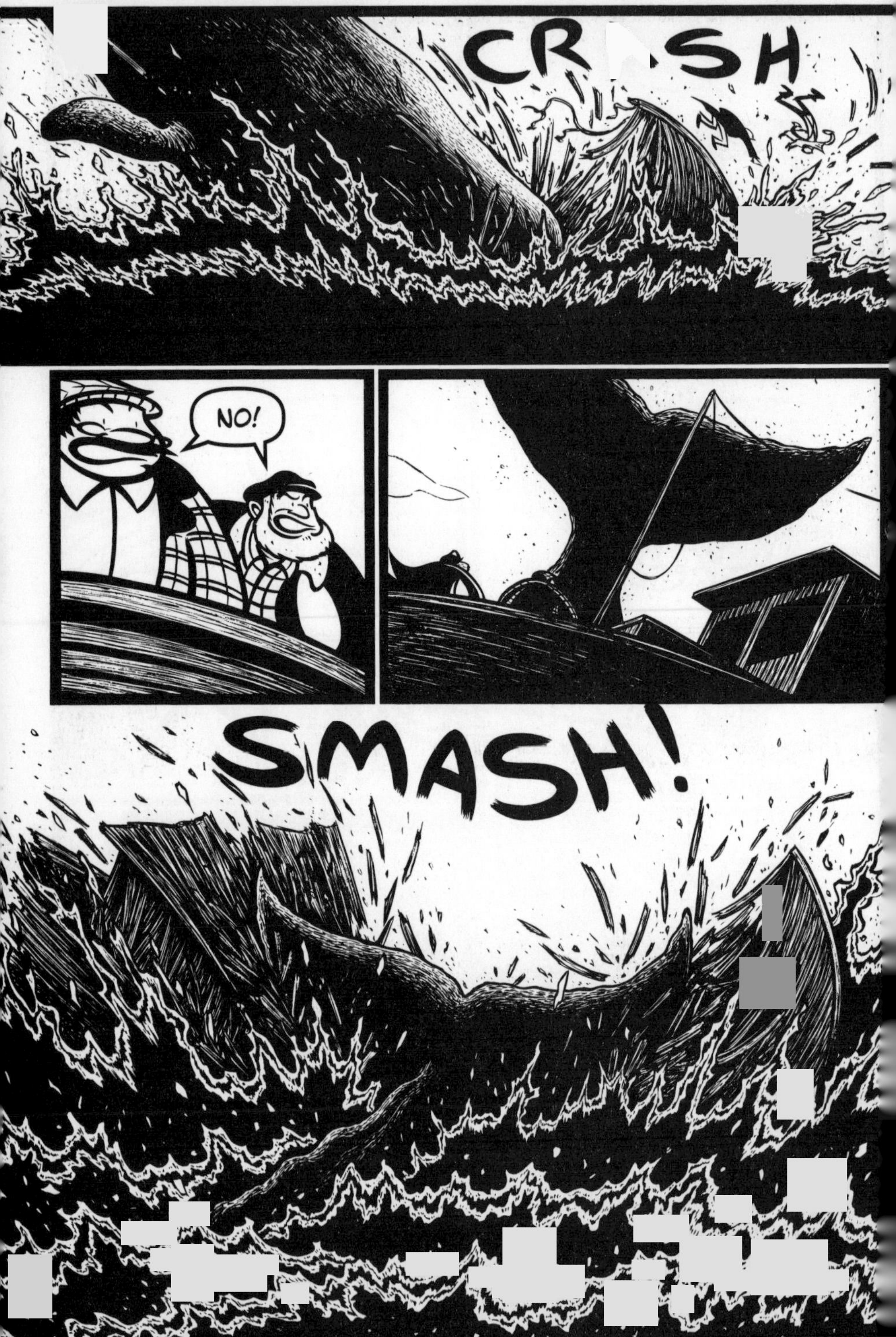
CRASH
NO!
SMASH!

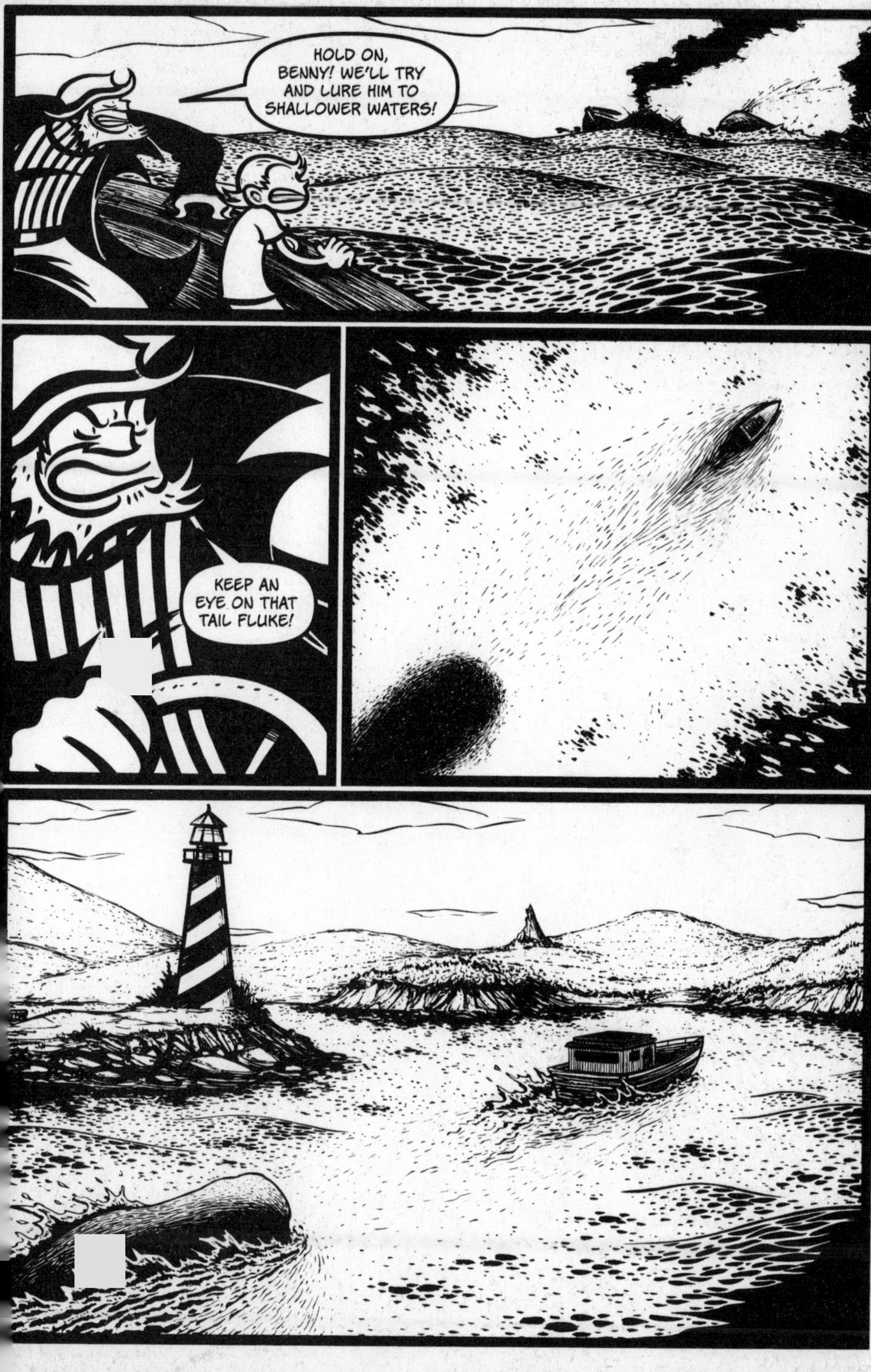
HOLD ON, BENNY! WE'LL TRY AND LURE HIM TO SHALLOWER WATERS!
KEEP AN EYE ON THAT TAIL FLUKE!

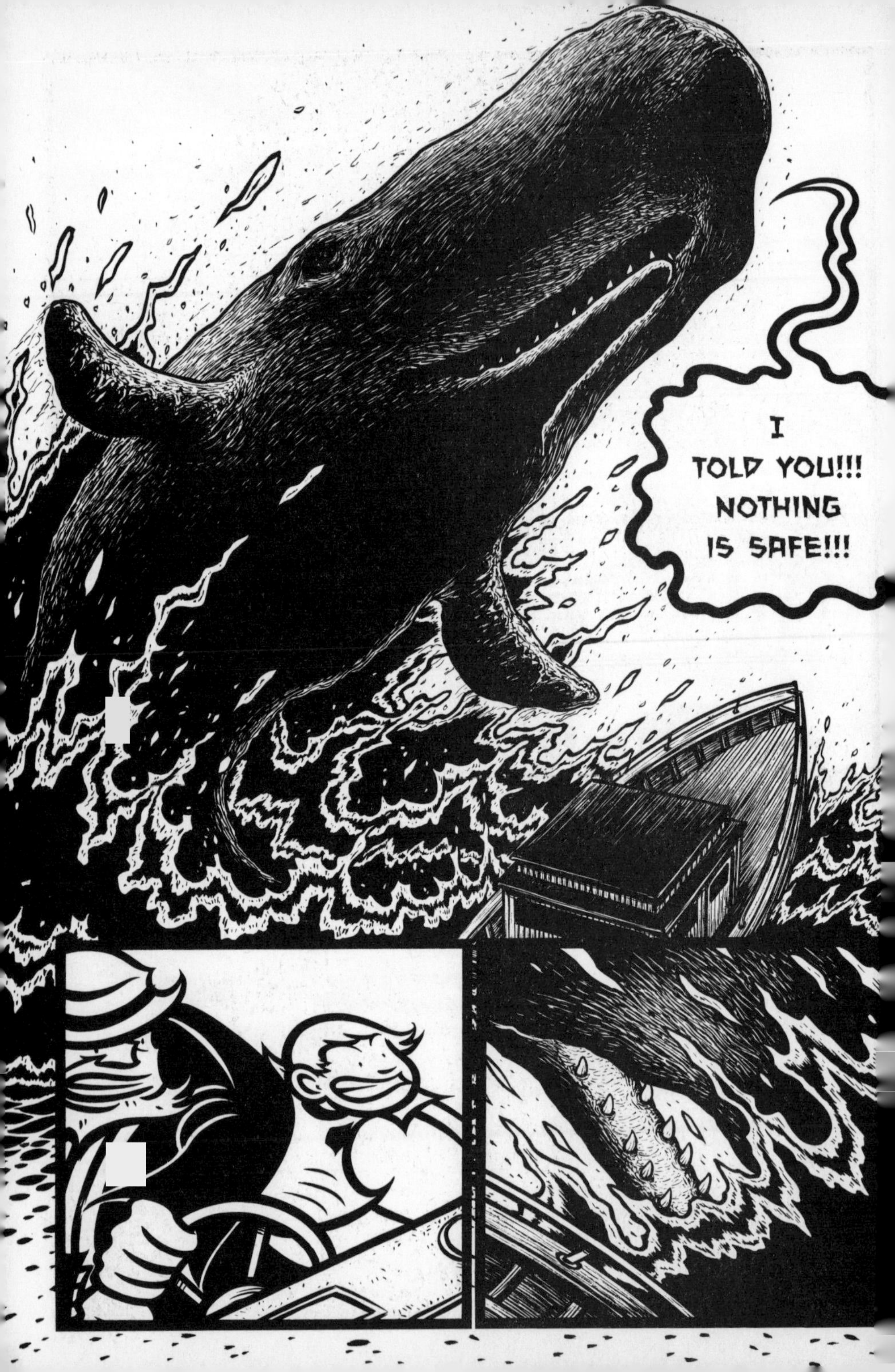
I TOLD YOU!!! NOTHING IS SAFE!!!

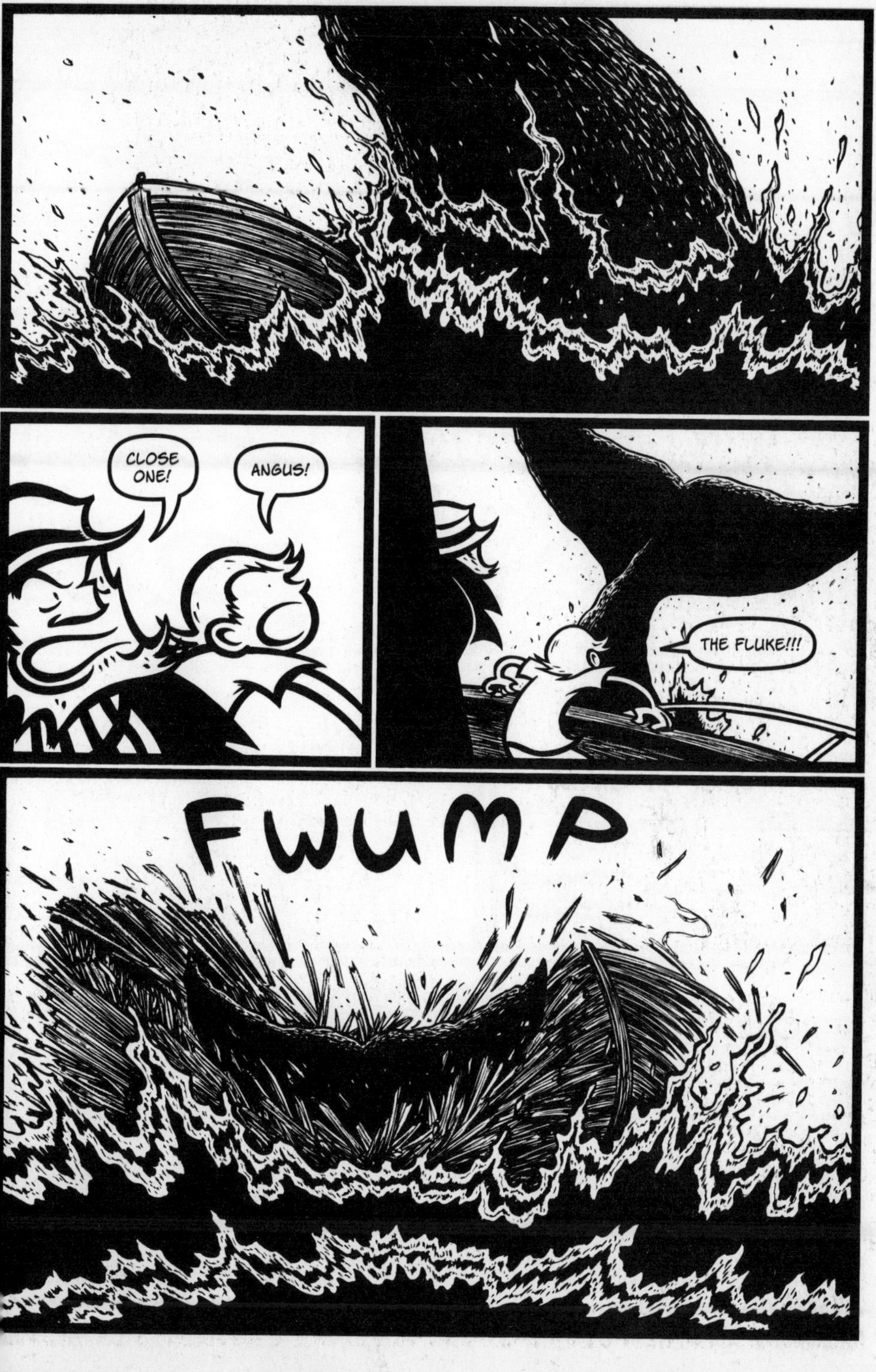
CLOSE ONE!
ANGUS!
THE FLUKE!!!
FWUMP

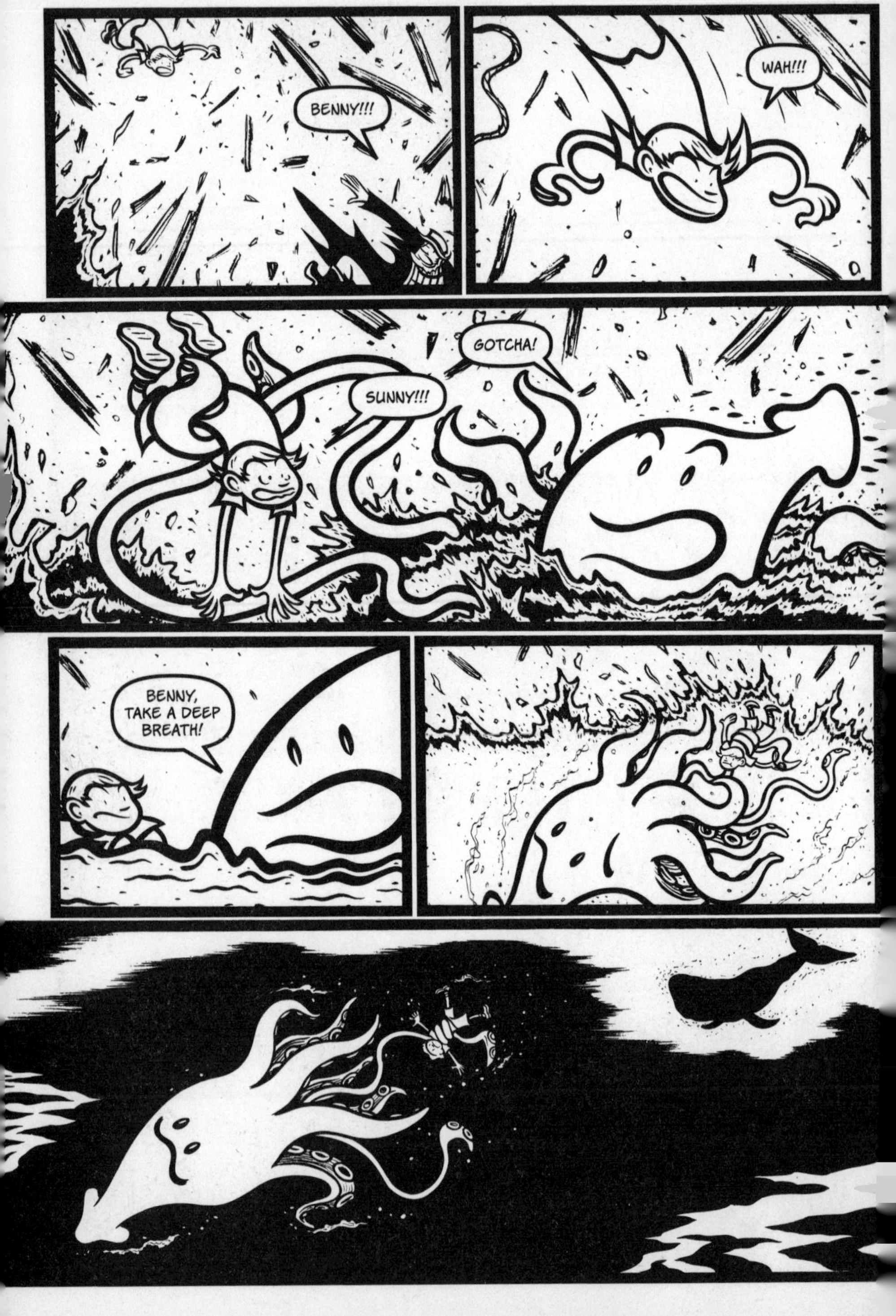
BENNY!!!
WAH!!!
GOTCHA!
SUNNY!!!
BENNY, TAKE A DEEP BREATH!

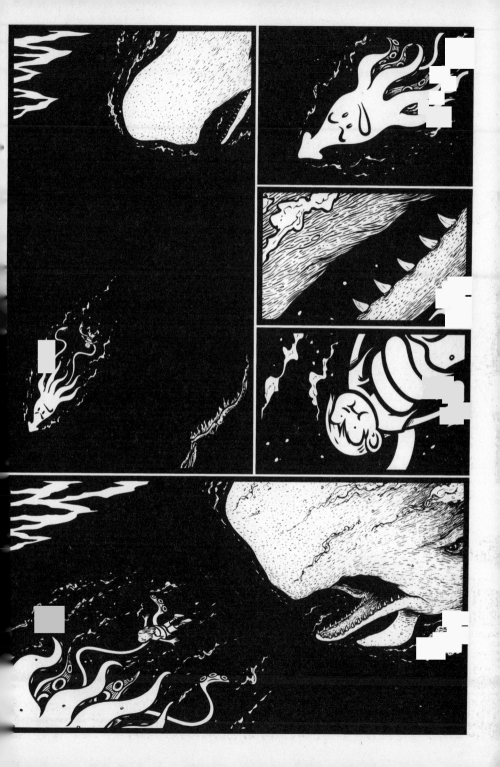

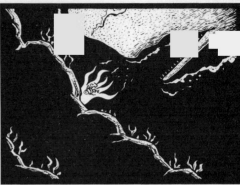

SMASH!

GRRRRR

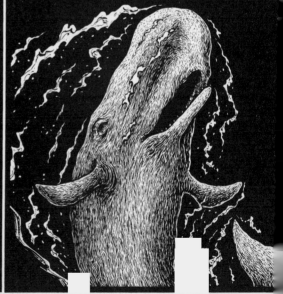

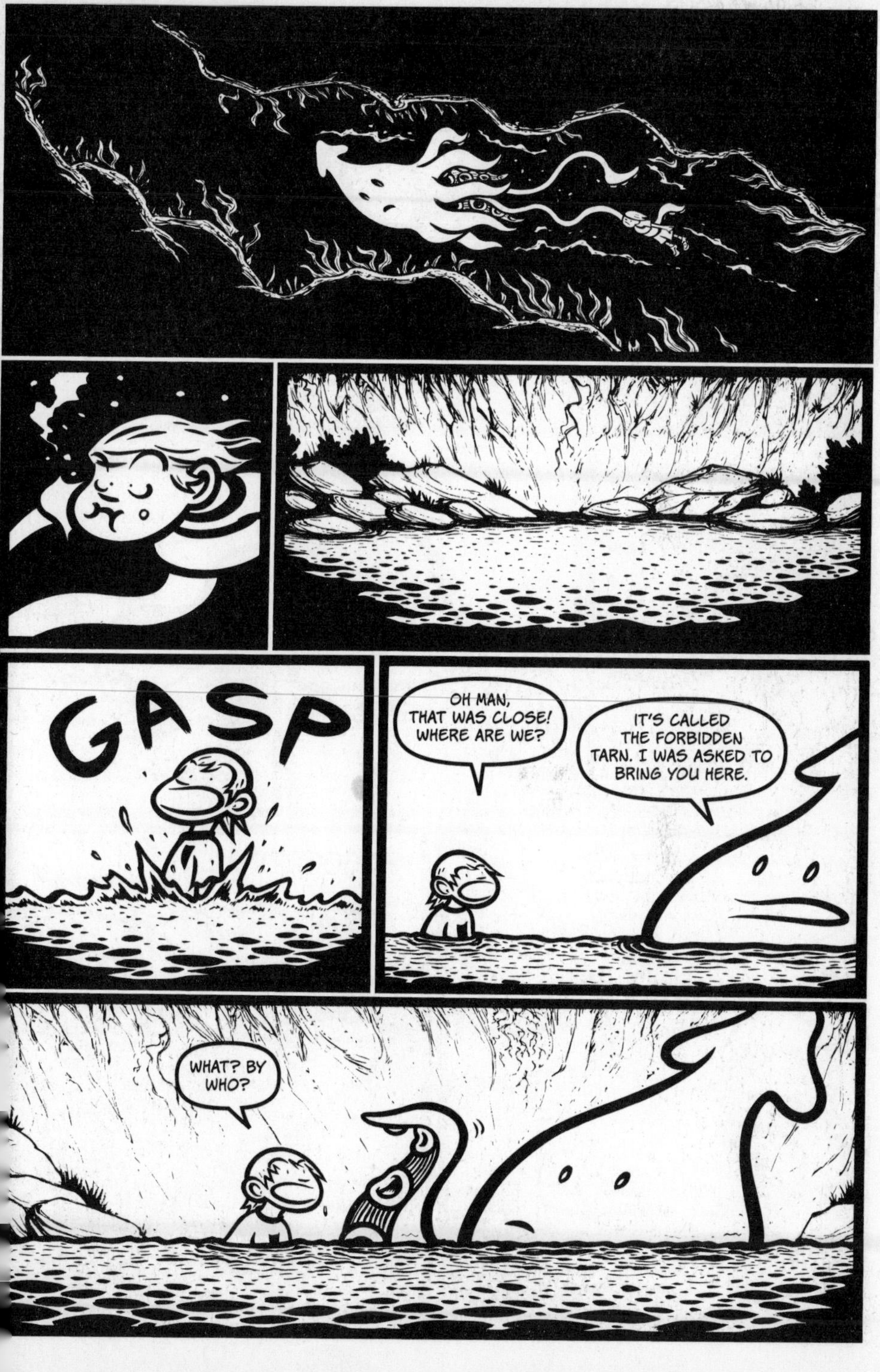
GASP
OH MAN, THAT WAS CLOSE! WHERE ARE WE?
IT'S CALLED THE FORBIDDEN TARN. I WAS ASKED TO BRING YOU HERE.
WHAT? BY WHO?

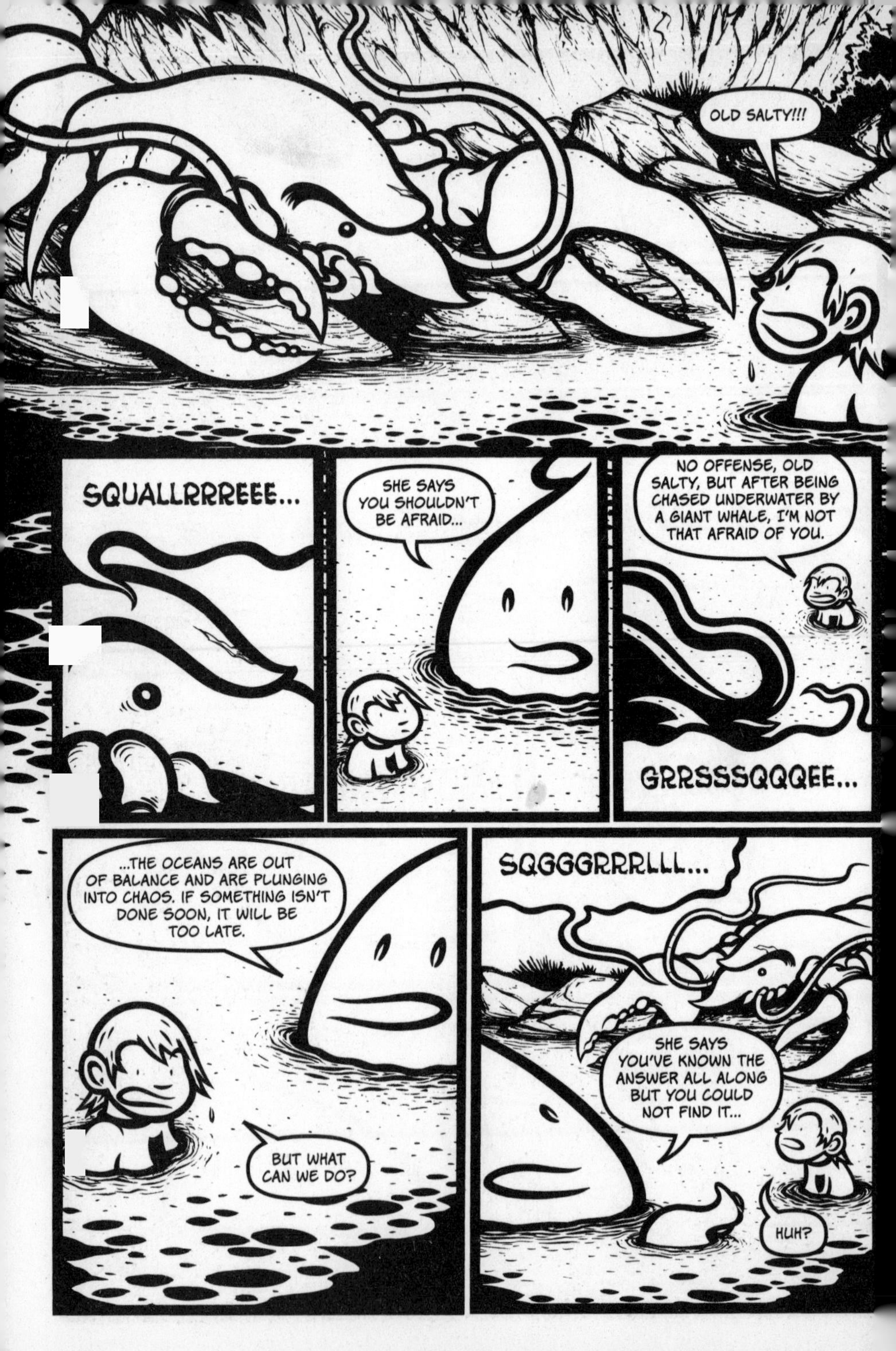
OLD SALTY!!!
SQUALLRRREEE...
SHE SAYS YOU SHOULDN'T BE AFRAID...
NO OFFENSE, OLD SALTY, BUT AFTER BEING CHASED UNDERWATER BY A GIANT WHALE, I'M NOT THAT AFRAID OF YOU.
GRRSSSQQQEE...
...THE OCEANS ARE OUT OF BALANCE AND ARE PLUNGING INTO CHAOS. IF SOMETHING ISN'T DONE SOON, IT WILL BE TOO LATE.
BUT WHAT CAN WE DO?
SQGGGRRRLLL...
SHE SAYS YOU'VE KNOWN THE ANSWER ALL ALONG BUT YOU COULD NOT FIND IT...
HUH?

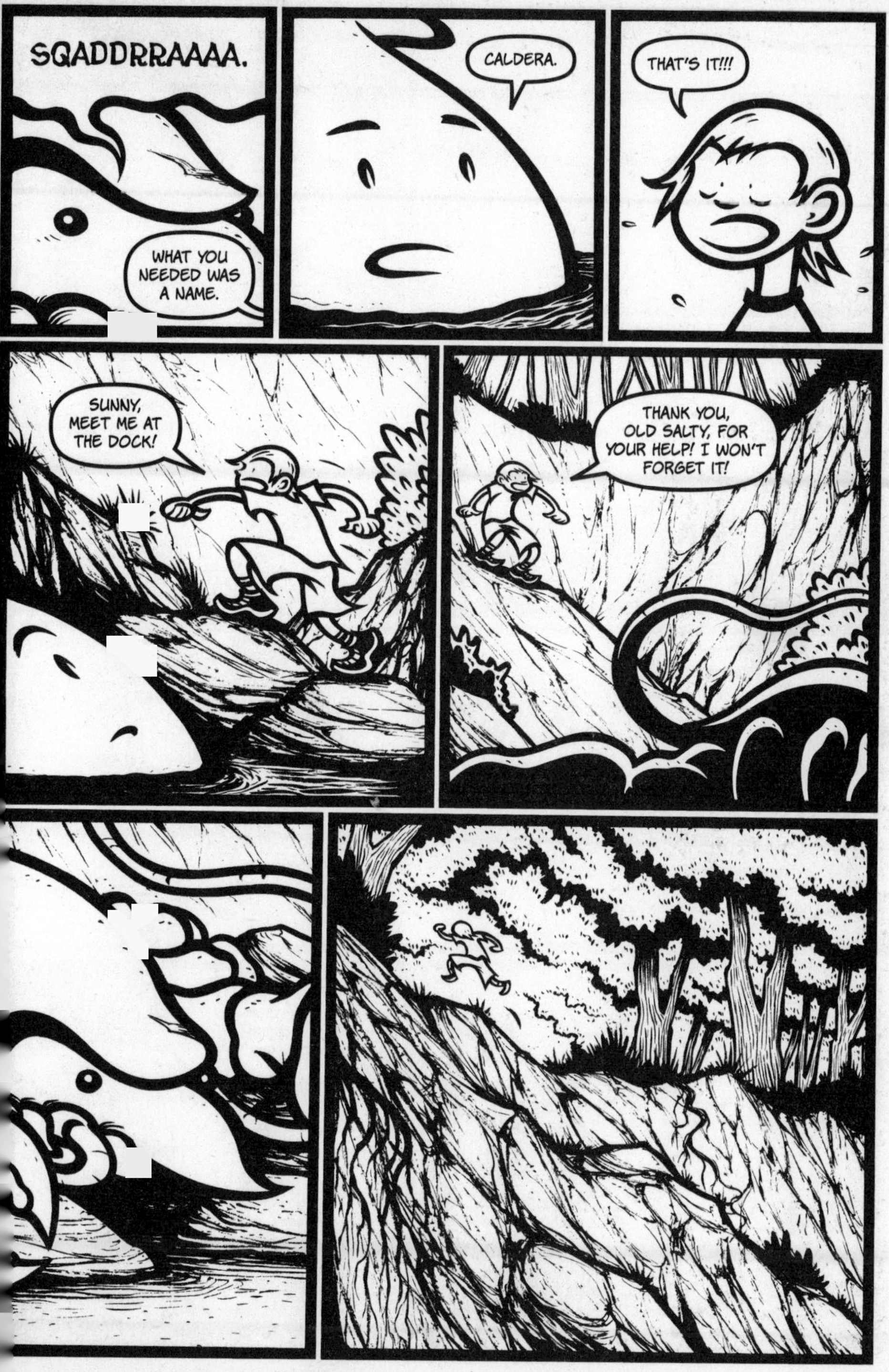
SQADDRRAAAA.
WHAT YOU NEEDED WAS A NAME.
CALDERA.
THAT'S IT!!!
SUNNY, MEET ME AT THE DOCK!
THANK YOU, OLD SALTY, FOR YOUR HELP! I WON'T FORGET IT!

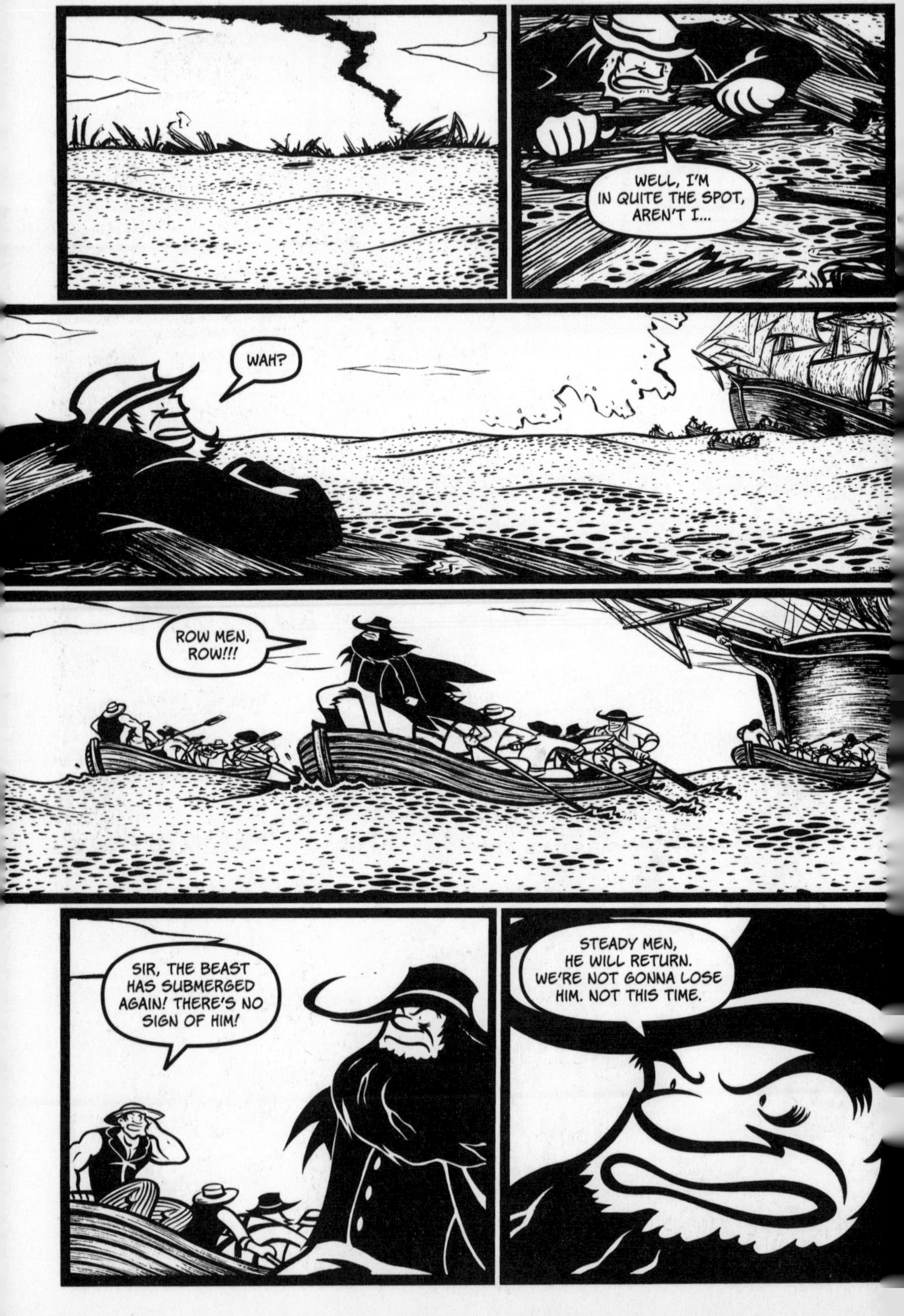
WELL, I'M IN QUITE THE SPOT, AREN'T I...
WAH?
ROW MEN, ROW!!!
SIR, THE BEAST HAS SUBMERGED AGAIN! THERE'S NO SIGN OF HIM!
STEADY MEN, HE WILL RETURN. WE'RE NOT GONNA LOSE HIM. NOT THIS TIME.

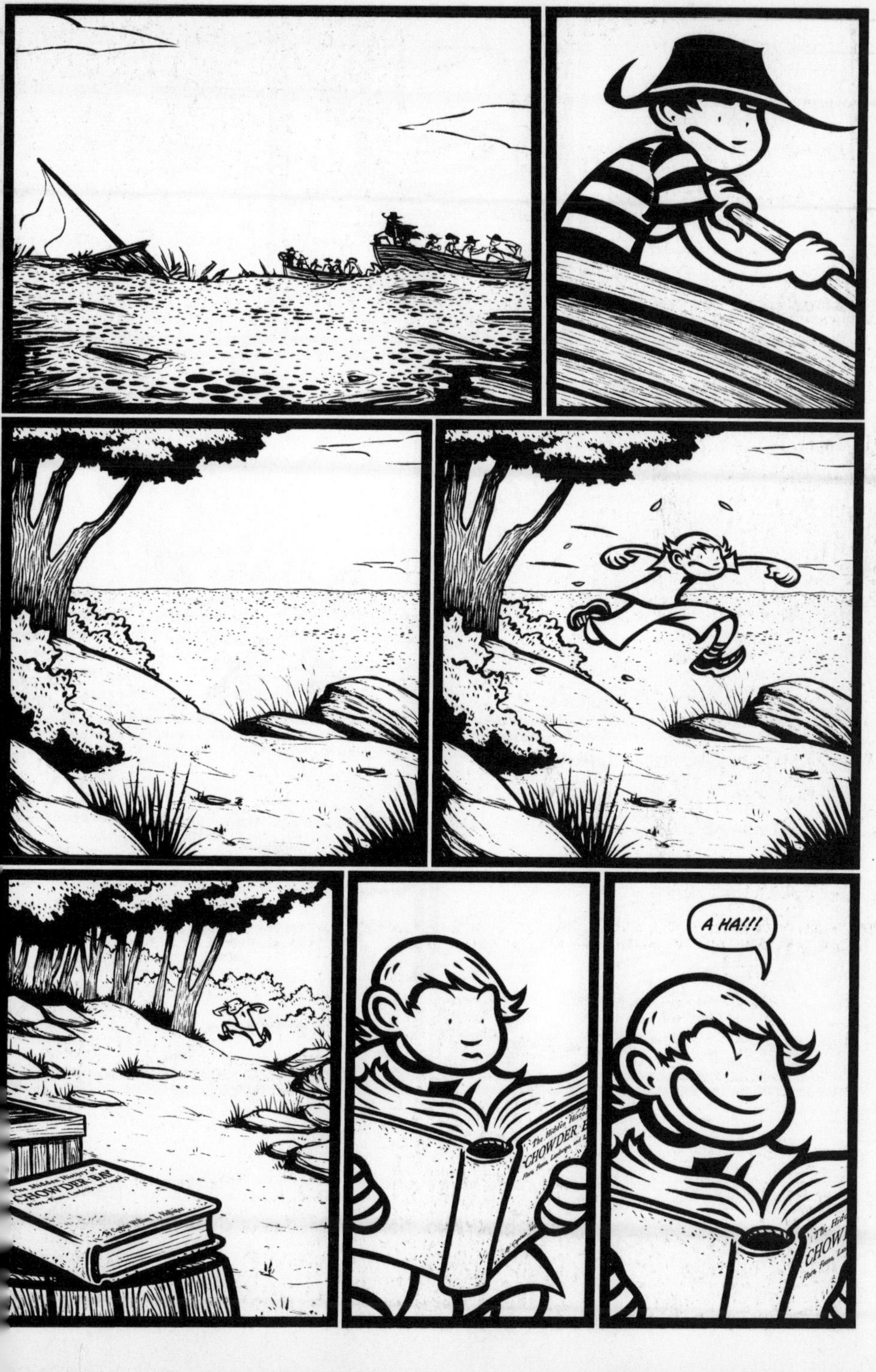
The Hidden History of
CHOWDER BAY
Flora, Fauna, Landscape, and Legend
A HA!!!

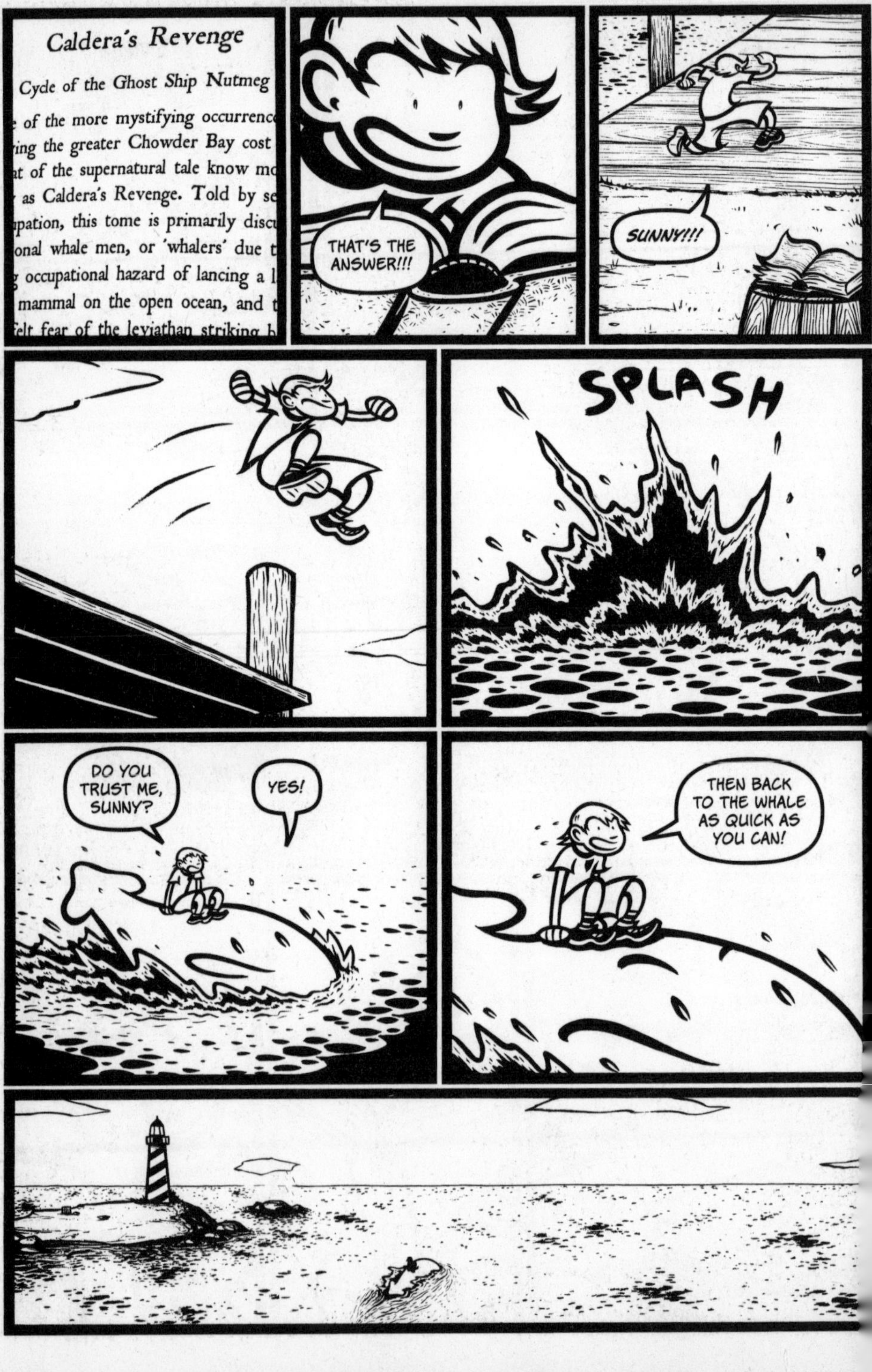
Caldera's Revenge
Cycle of the Ghost Ship Nutmeg
of the more mystifying occurrenc
ing the greater Chowder Bay cost
t of the supernatural tale know m
as Caldera's Revenge. Told by se
pation, this tome is primarily disc
onal whale men, or 'whalers' due t
occupational hazard of lancing a l
mammal on the open ocean, and t
elt fear of the leviathan striking b
THAT'S THE ANSWER!!!
SUNNY!!!
SPLASH
DO YOU TRUST ME, SUNNY?
YES!
THEN BACK TO THE WHALE AS QUICK AS YOU CAN!

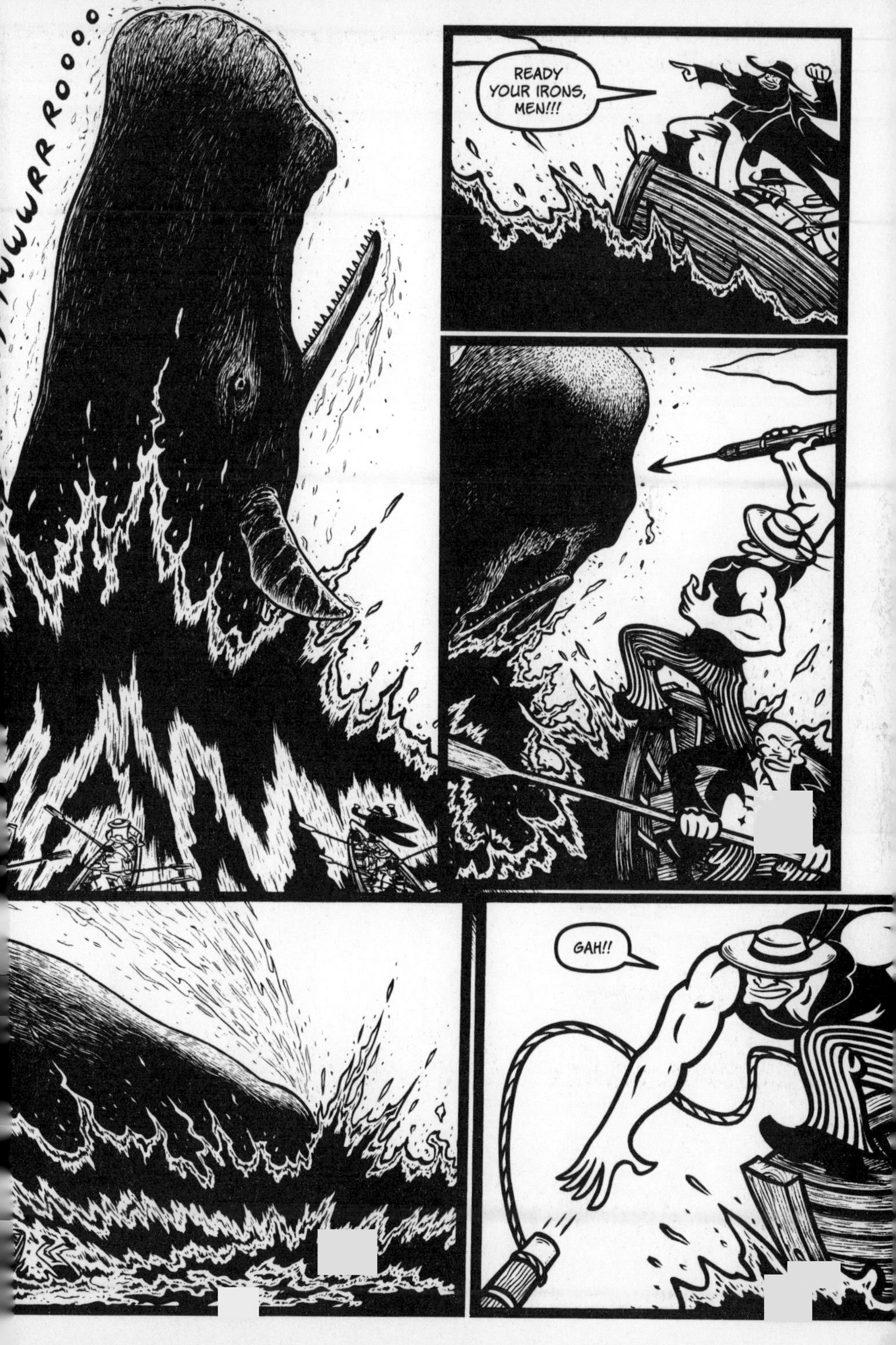
WWWRR ROOOO
READY YOUR IRONS, MEN!!!
GAH!!

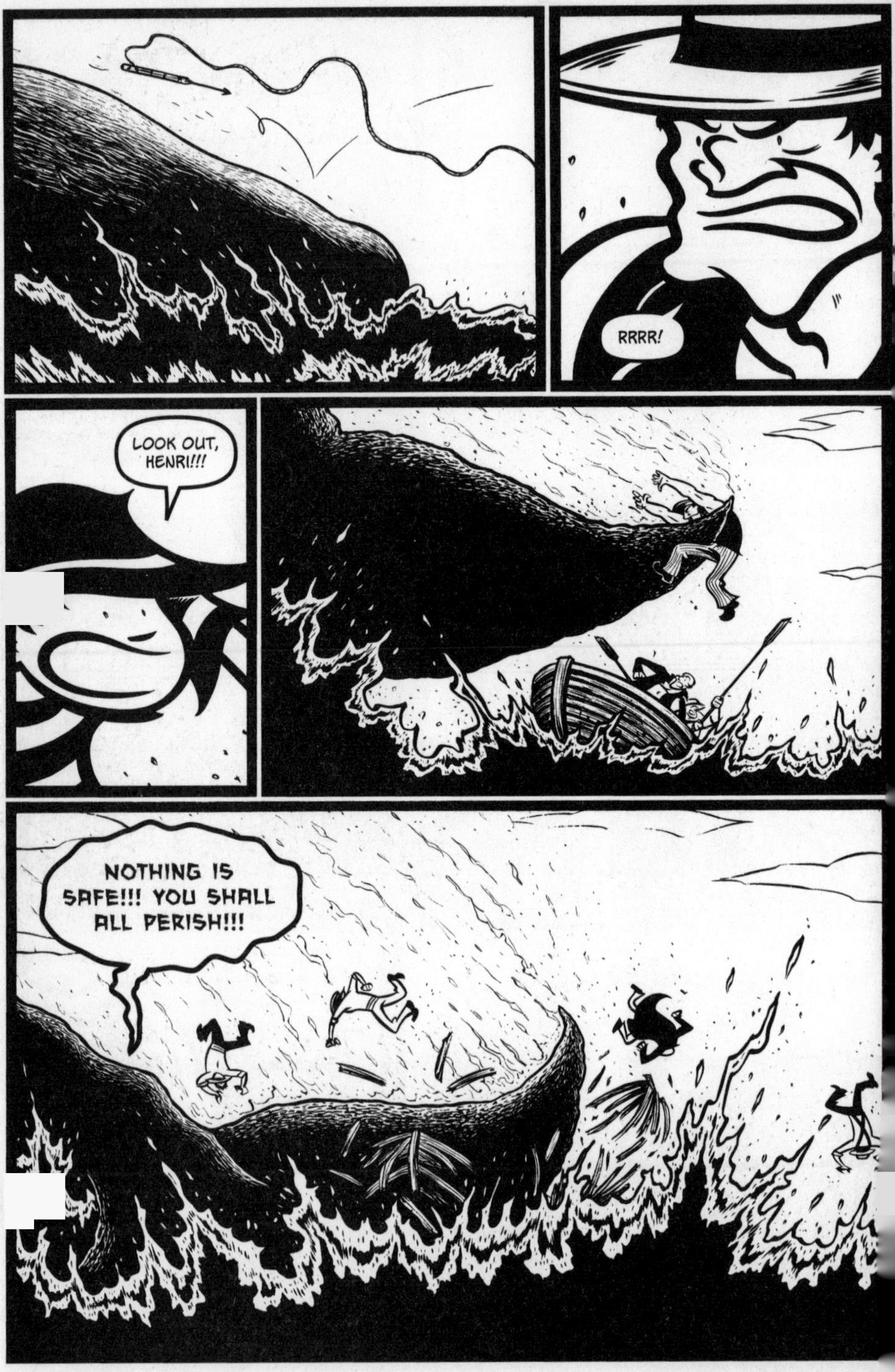
RRRR!
LOOK OUT, HENRI!!!
NOTHING IS SAFE!!! YOU SHALL ALL PERISH!!!

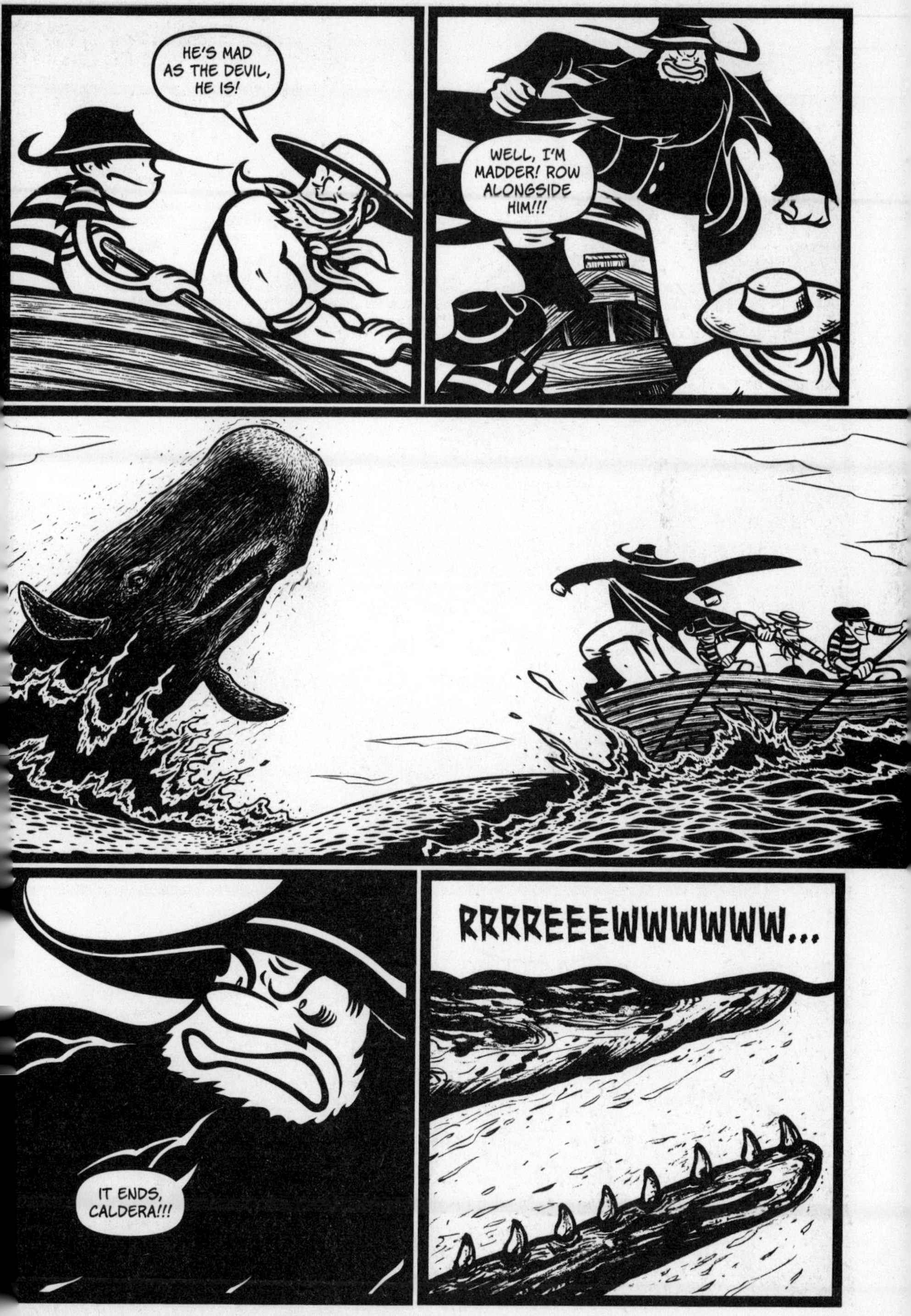
HE'S MAD AS THE DEVIL, HE IS!
WELL, I'M MADDER! ROW ALONGSIDE HIM!!!
IT ENDS, CALDERA!!!
RRRREEEWWWWWW...

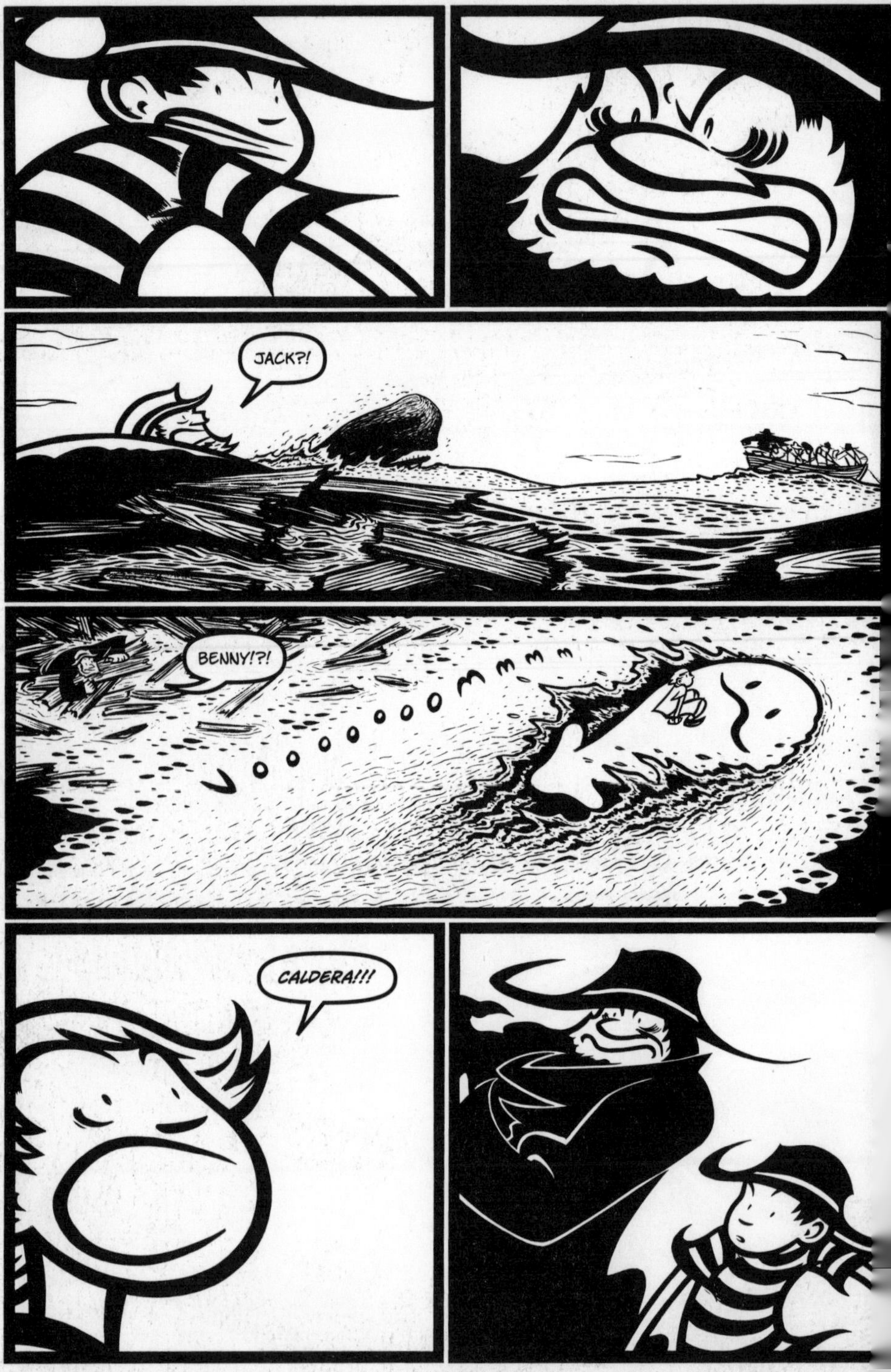
JACK?!
BENNY!?!
VOOOOOOMMMM
CALDERA!!!

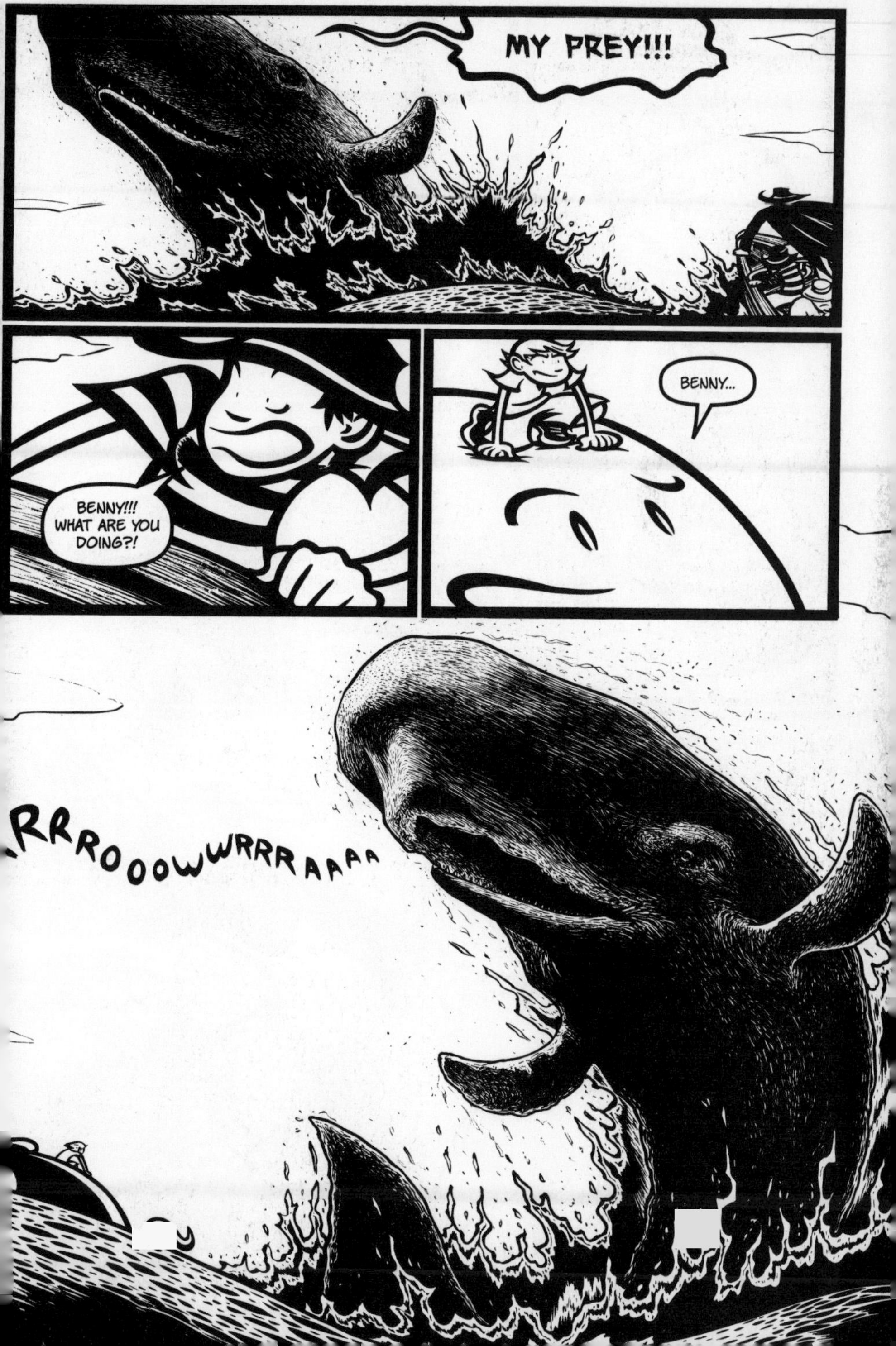
MY PREY!!!
BENNY!!! WHAT ARE YOU DOING?!
BENNY...
RRROOOOWWRRRAAAA

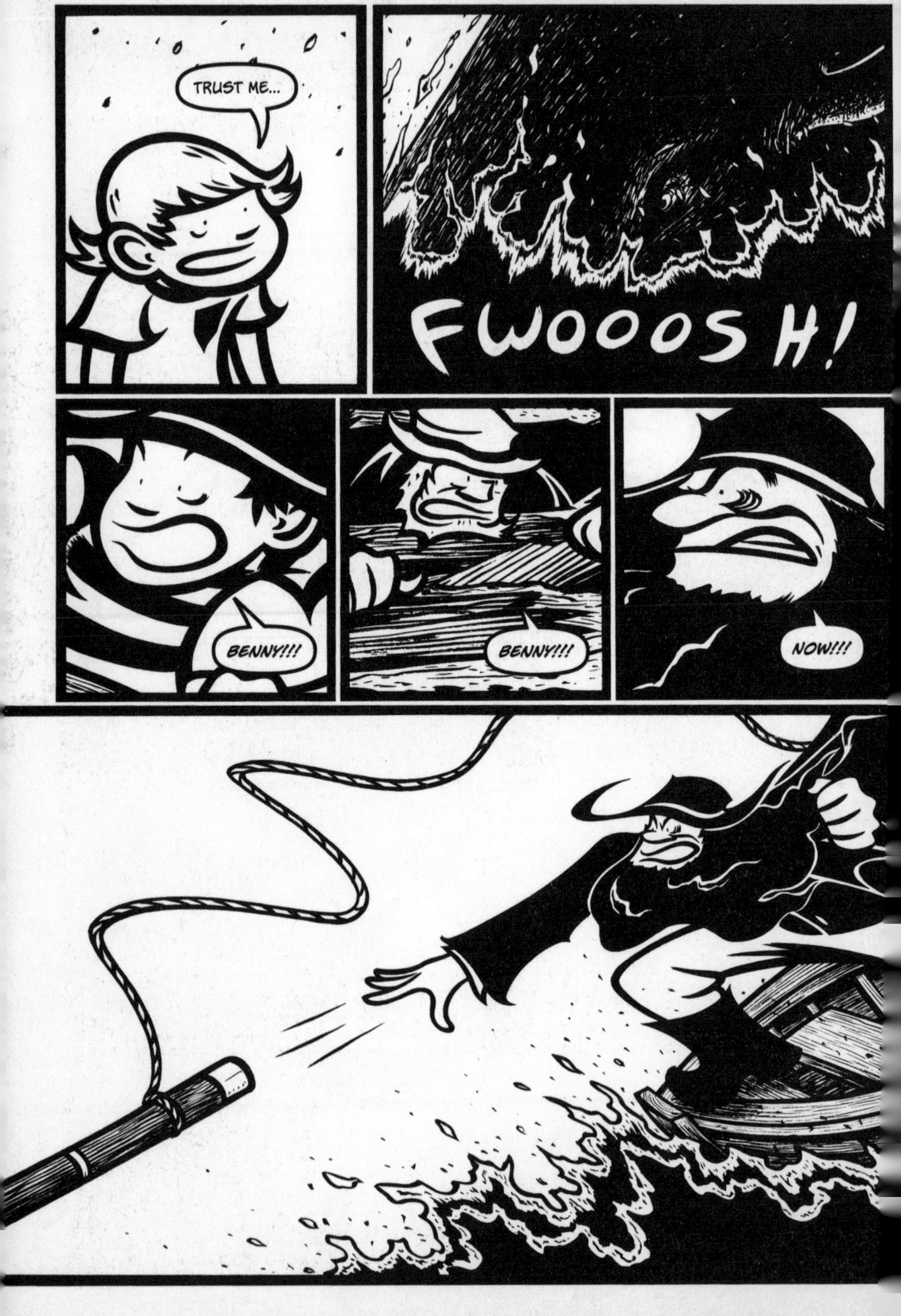
TRUST ME...
FWOOOSH!
BENNY!!!
BENNY!!!
NOW!!!

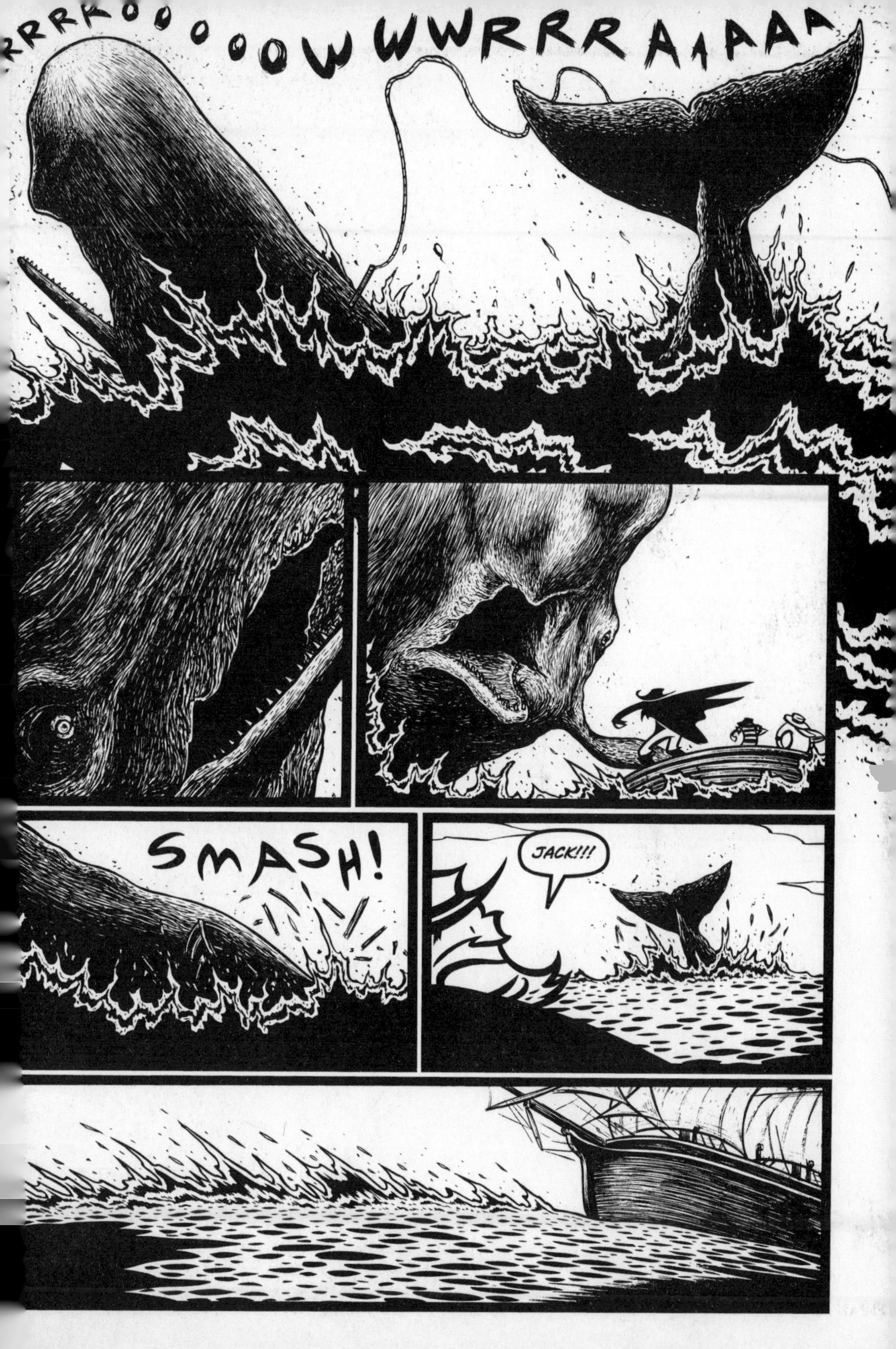
RRRROOOOOOWWWRRRRAAAA
SMASH!
JACK!!!

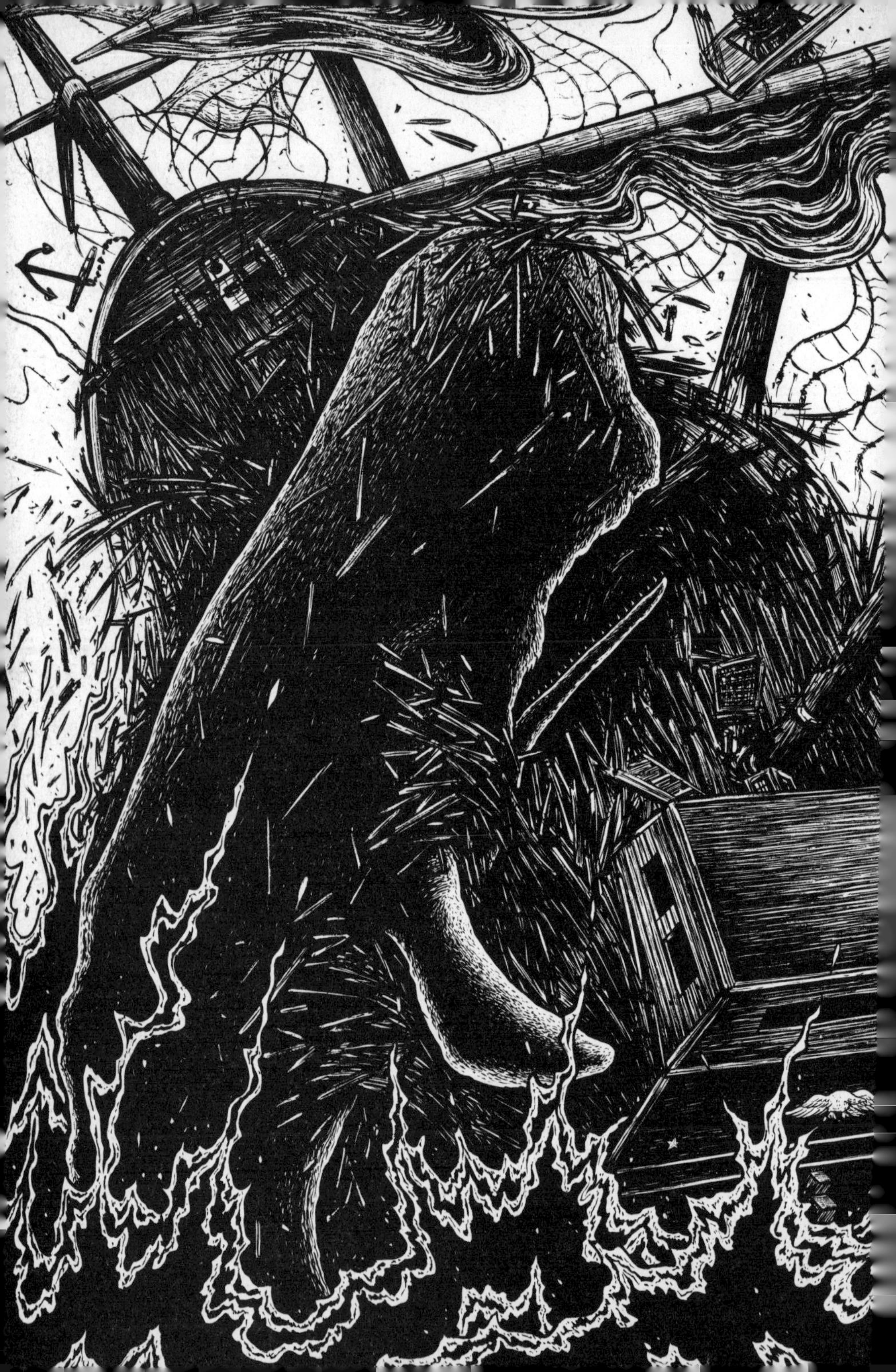

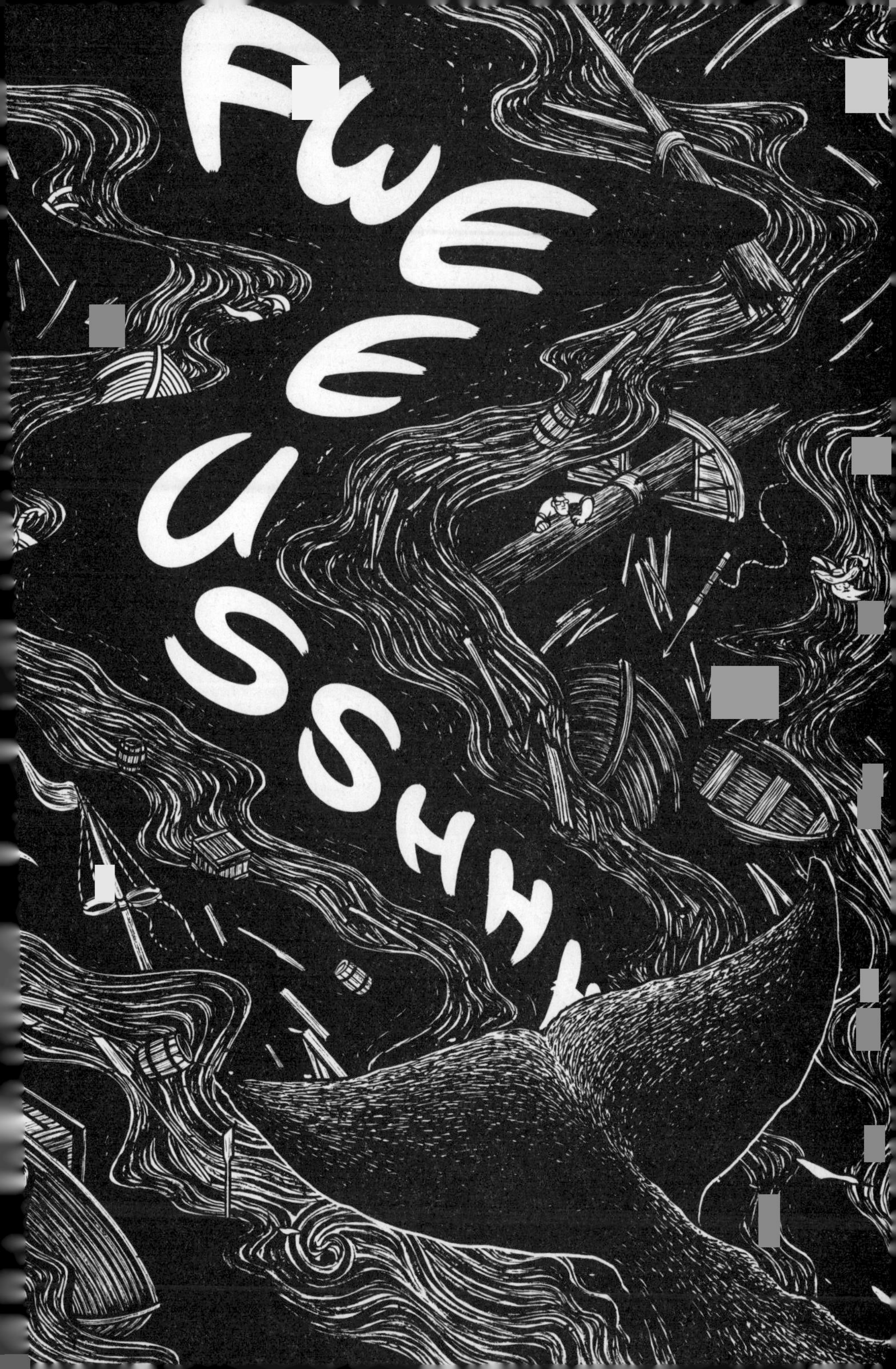
AWEEUSSHH

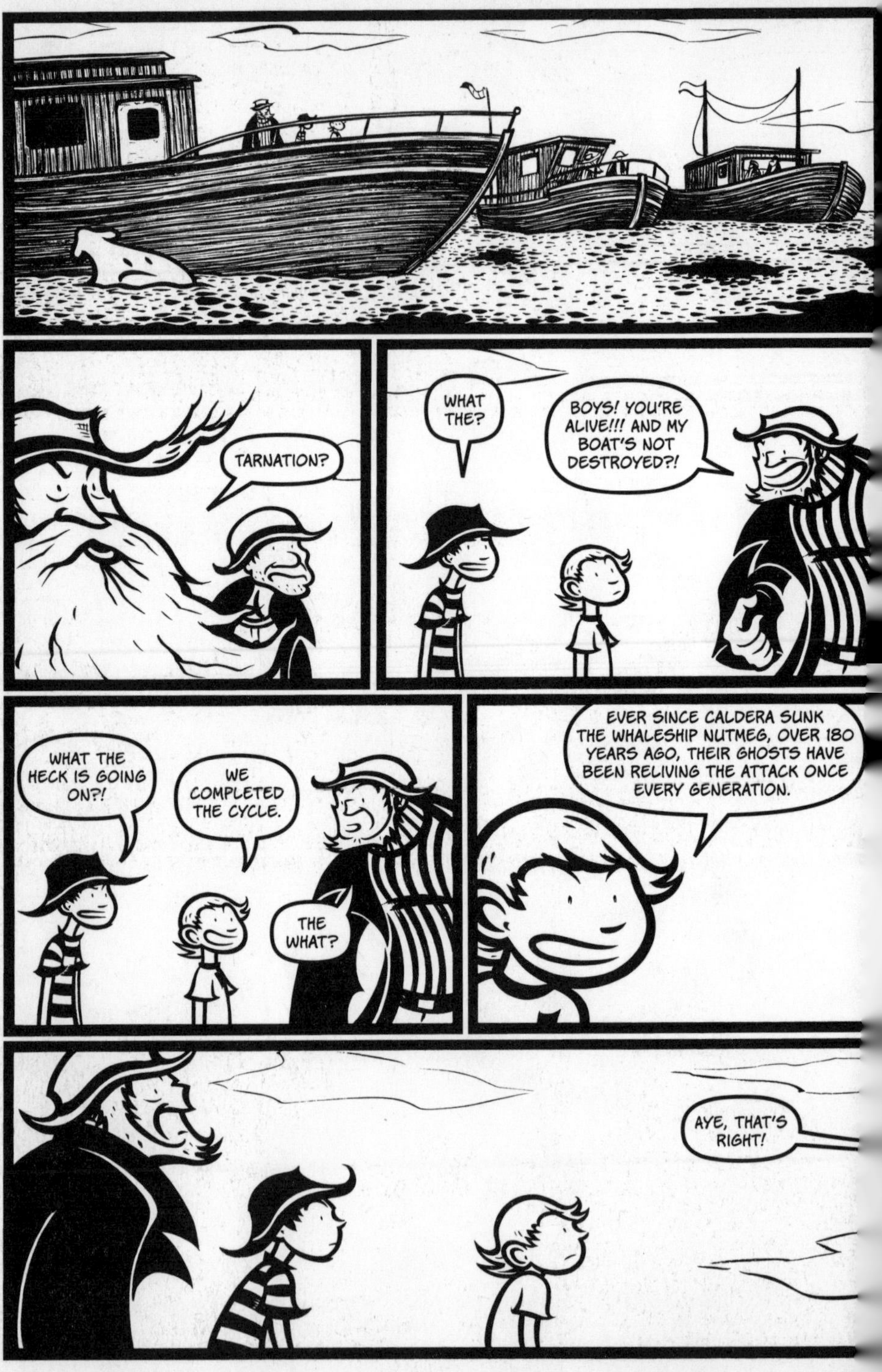
TARNATION?
WHAT THE?
BOYS! YOU'RE ALIVE!!! AND MY BOAT'S NOT DESTROYED?!
WHAT THE HECK IS GOING ON?!
WE COMPLETED THE CYCLE.
THE WHAT?
EVER SINCE CALDERA SUNK THE WHALESHIP NUTMEG, OVER 180 YEARS AGO, THEIR GHOSTS HAVE BEEN RELIVING THE ATTACK ONCE EVERY GENERATION.
AYE, THAT'S RIGHT!

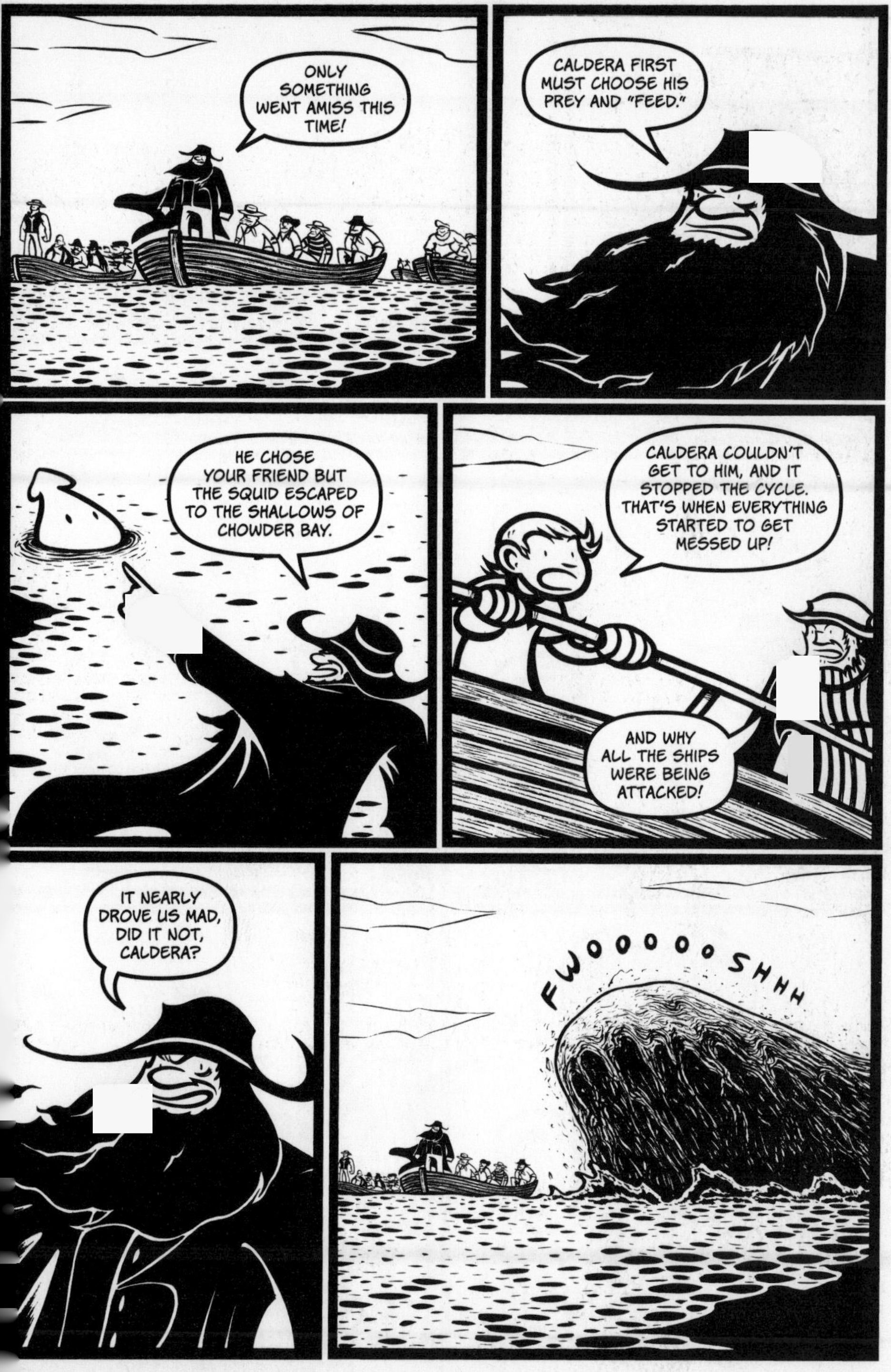
ONLY SOMETHING WENT AMISS THIS TIME!
CALDERA FIRST MUST CHOOSE HIS PREY AND "FEED."
HE CHOSE YOUR FRIEND BUT THE SQUID ESCAPED TO THE SHALLOWS OF CHOWDER BAY.
CALDERA COULDN'T GET TO HIM, AND IT STOPPED THE CYCLE. THAT'S WHEN EVERYTHING STARTED TO GET MESSED UP!
AND WHY ALL THE SHIPS WERE BEING ATTACKED!
IT NEARLY DROVE US MAD, DID IT NOT, CALDERA?
FWOOOOOSHHH

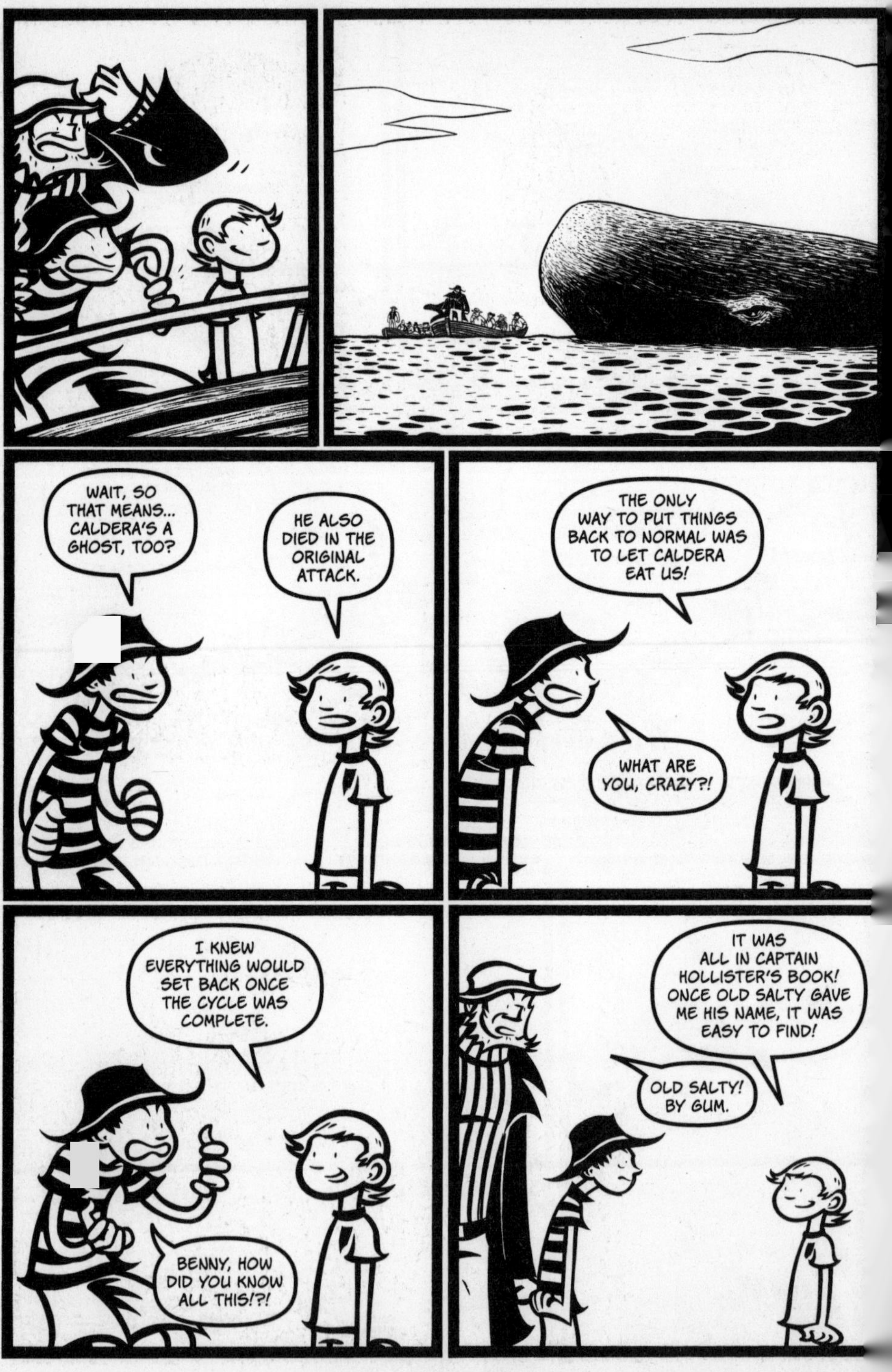
WAIT, SO THAT MEANS... CALDERA'S A GHOST, TOO?
HE ALSO DIED IN THE ORIGINAL ATTACK.
THE ONLY WAY TO PUT THINGS BACK TO NORMAL WAS TO LET CALDERA EAT US!
WHAT ARE YOU, CRAZY?!
I KNEW EVERYTHING WOULD SET BACK ONCE THE CYCLE WAS COMPLETE.
BENNY, HOW DID YOU KNOW ALL THIS!?!
IT WAS ALL IN CAPTAIN HOLLISTER'S BOOK! ONCE OLD SALTY GAVE ME HIS NAME, IT WAS EASY TO FIND!
OLD SALTY! BY GUM.

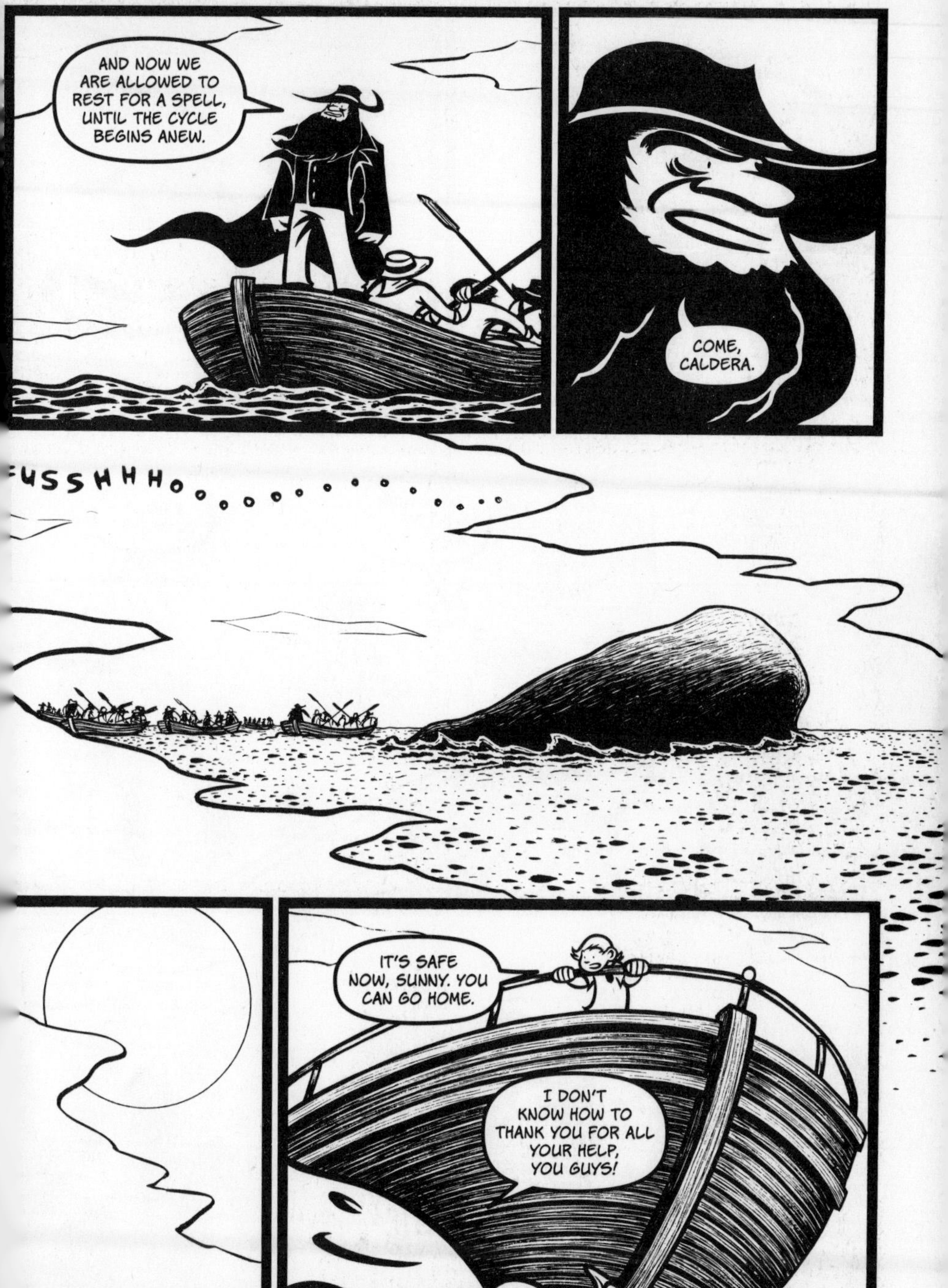
AND NOW WE ARE ALLOWED TO REST FOR A SPELL, UNTIL THE CYCLE BEGINS ANEW.
COME, CALDERA.
FUSSHHHO.........
IT'S SAFE NOW, SUNNY. YOU CAN GO HOME.
I DON'T KNOW HOW TO THANK YOU FOR ALL YOUR HELP, YOU GUYS!

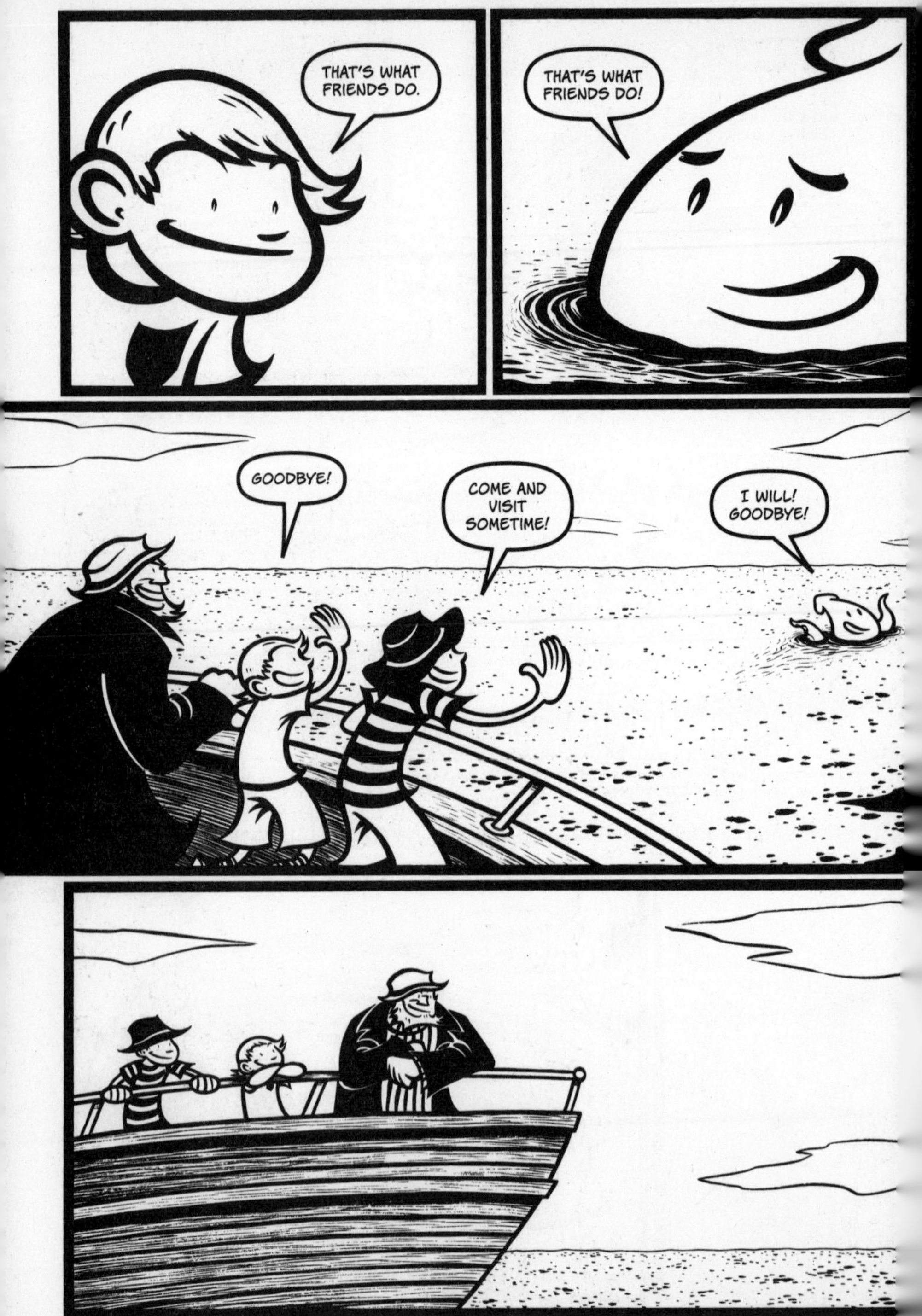
THAT'S WHAT FRIENDS DO.
THAT'S WHAT FRIENDS DO!
GOODBYE!
COME AND VISIT SOMETIME!
I WILL! GOODBYE!

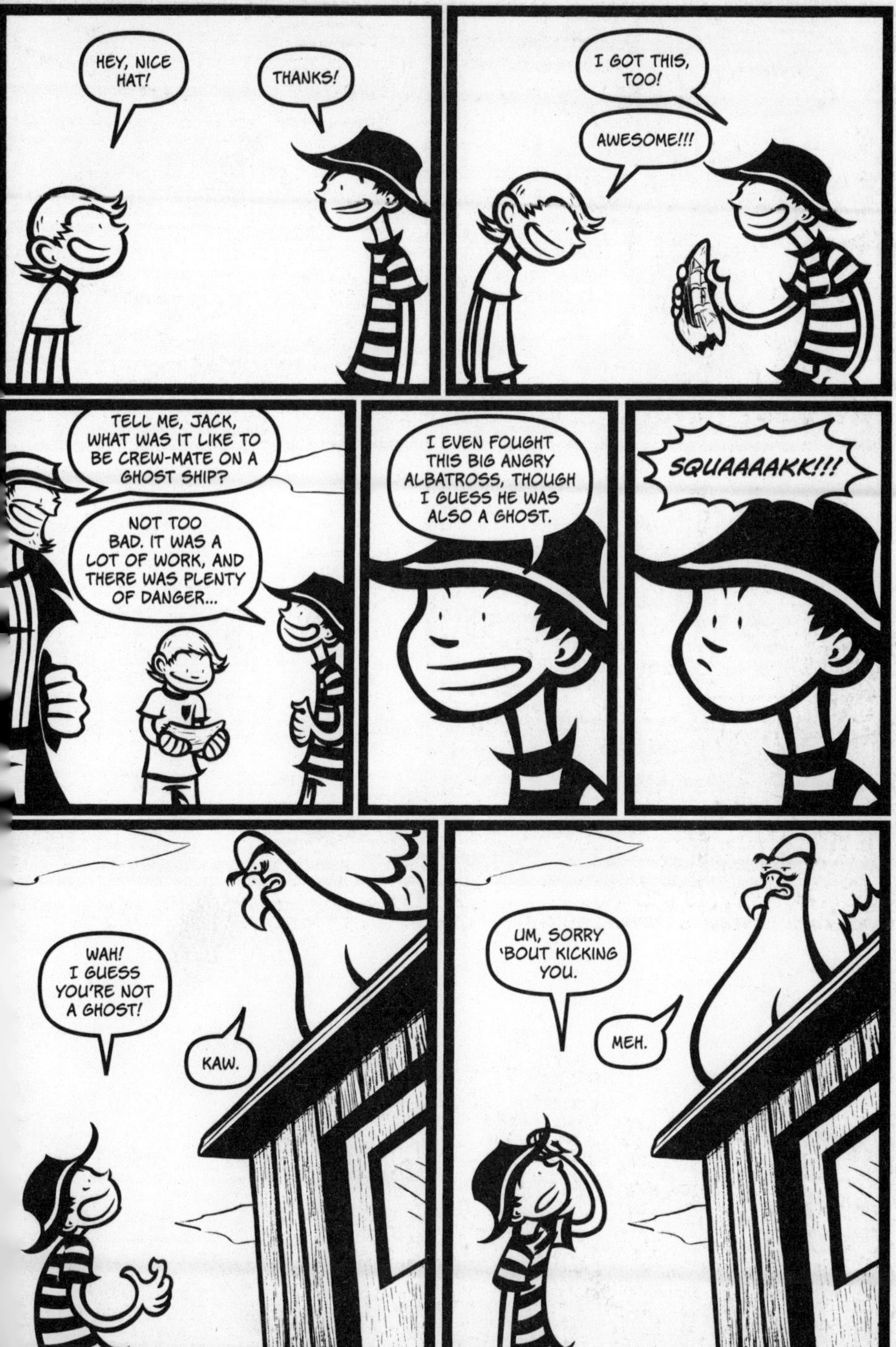
HEY, NICE HAT!
THANKS!
I GOT THIS, TOO!
AWESOME!!!
TELL ME, JACK, WHAT WAS IT LIKE TO BE CREW-MATE ON A GHOST SHIP?
NOT TOO BAD. IT WAS A LOT OF WORK, AND THERE WAS PLENTY OF DANGER...
I EVEN FOUGHT THIS BIG ANGRY ALBATROSS, THOUGH I GUESS HE WAS ALSO A GHOST.
SQUAAAAKK!!!
WAH! I GUESS YOU'RE NOT A GHOST!
KAW.
UM, SORRY 'BOUT KICKING YOU.
MEH.

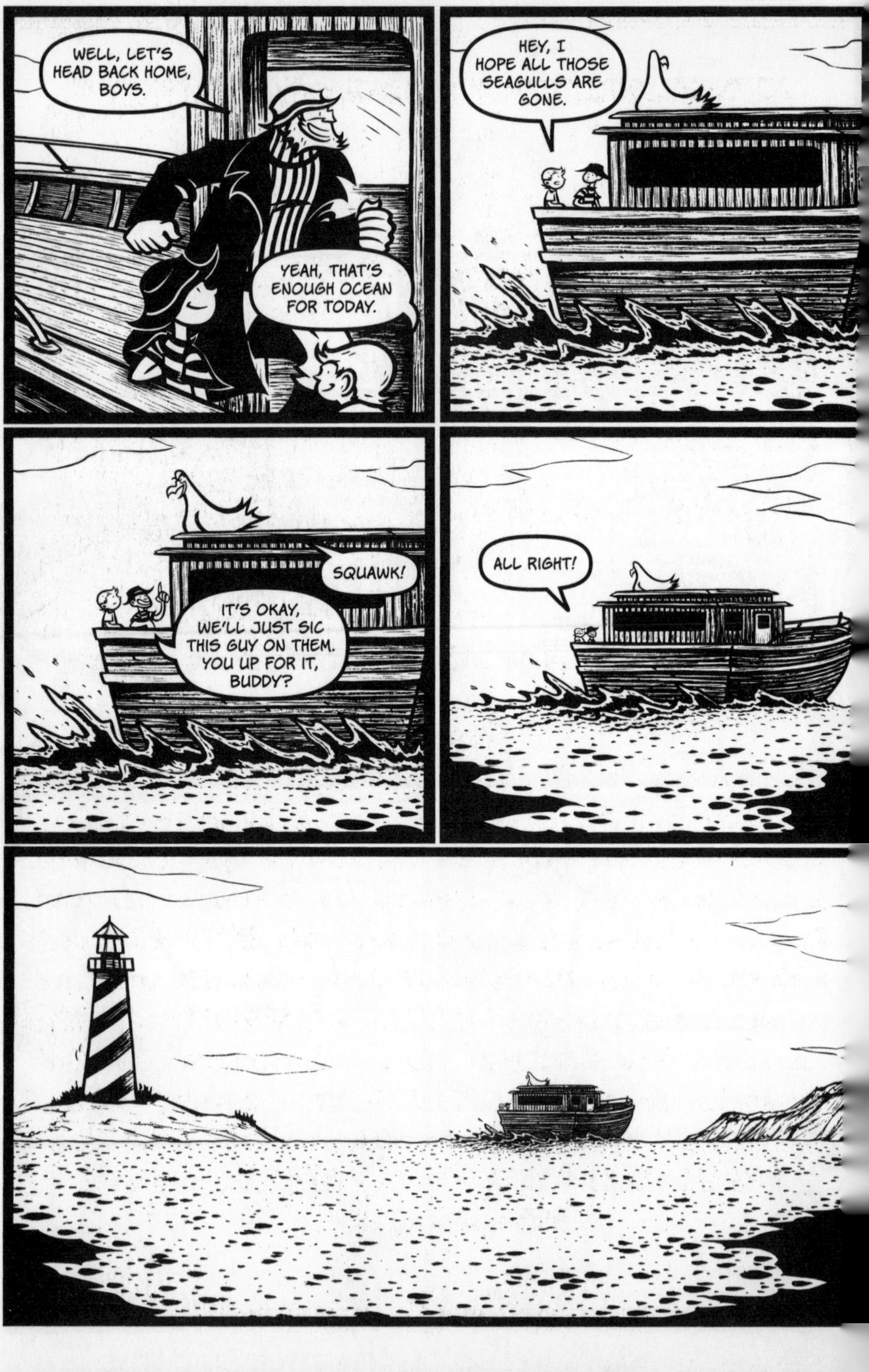
WELL, LET'S HEAD BACK HOME, BOYS.
YEAH, THAT'S ENOUGH OCEAN FOR TODAY.
HEY, I HOPE ALL THOSE SEAGULLS ARE GONE.
SQUAWK!
IT'S OKAY, WE'LL JUST SIC THIS GUY ON THEM. YOU UP FOR IT, BUDDY?
ALL RIGHT!

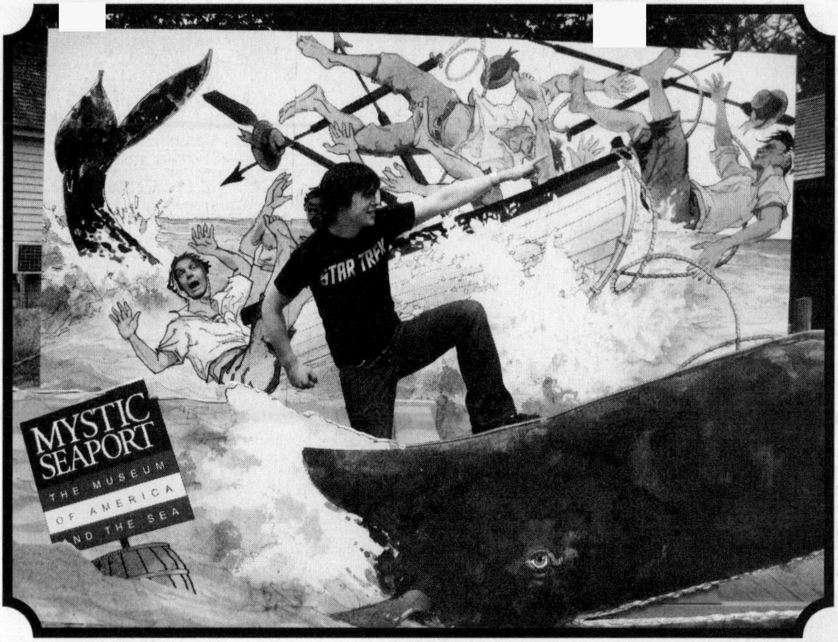
MYSTIC
SEAPORT
THE MUSEUM
OF AMERICA
AND THE SEA
STAR TREK

Matthew Loux was born in Norwich, Connecticut and graduated from the School of Visual Arts, NYC, in 2001. He went on a whale watch as a kid where he got to see a humpback whale up close, and like many, is mildly preoccupied by the squid and whale diorama at the American Museum of Natural History (though his favorite is the T-Rex and Giant Ground Sloth skeleton). Matthew created the comic series SALT WATER TAFFY which was inspired by his youth spent in the New England countryside as well as vacationing in and around Maine with his family. In addition to the SALT WATER TAFFY series, Matthew also created the graphic novel SIDESCROLLERS, illustrated the graphic novel F-STOP, and illustrated the board comic GOOD NIGHT GABBALAND based on the popular TV program YO GABBA GABBA! Matthew was also the inker of the comic, STAR WARS ADVENTURES, HAN SOLO AND THE HOLLOW MOON OF KHORYA published by Dark Horse comics. Matthew resides in Brooklyn, NY.

OTHER BOOKS FROM MATTHEW LOUX...

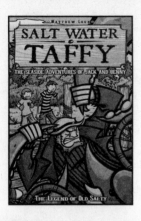

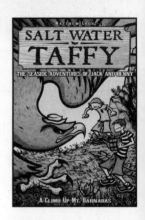

Matthew Loux
SALT WATER TAFFY
THE SEASIDE ADVENTURES OF JACK AND BENNY
The Legend of Old Salty

SALT WATER TAFFY, VOL. 1 – THE LEGEND OF OLD SALTY
By Matthew Loux
96 pages, digest, black & white
$5.99 US
ISBN: 978-1-932664-94-2

Matthew Loux
SALT WATER TAFFY
THE SEASIDE ADVENTURES OF JACK AND BENNY
A Climb Up Mt. Barnabas

SALT WATER TAFFY, VOL. 2 – A CLIMB UP MT. BARNABAS
By Matthew Loux
96 pages, digest, black & white
$5.99 US
ISBN: 978-1-934964-03-3

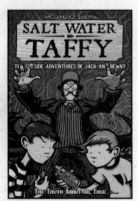

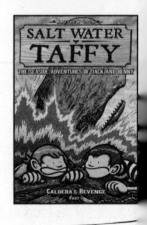

Matthew Loux
SALT WATER TAFFY
The Truth About Dr. True

SALT WATER TAFFY, VOL. 3 – THE TRUTH ABOUT DR. TRUE
By Matthew Loux
96 pages, digest, black & white
$5.99 US
ISBN 978-1-934964-04-0

Matthew Loux
SALT WATER TAFFY
THE SEASIDE ADVENTURES OF JACK AND BENNY
Caldera's Revenge
Part 1

SALT WATER TAFFY, VOL. 4 – CALDERA'S REVENGE
By Matthew Loux
96 pages, digest, black & white
$5.99 US
ISBN 978-1-934964-62-0

SIDESCROLLERS
Awesomevision

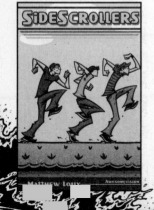

SIDESCROLLERS
By Matthew Loux
216 pages, digest, black & white
$11.95 US
ISBN 978-1-932664-50-8

Available at finer comics shops everywhere. For a comics store near you, call 1-888-COMIC-BOOK or visit www.comicshops.us. For more Oni Press titles and information visit www.onipress.com.

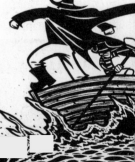